EMERGING COMPUTING TECHNIQUES IN SCIENCE

VOLUME 2

MATTHEW N. O. SADIKU

Emerging Computing Techniques In Science
VOLUME 2

Copyright © 2022 Matthew N. O. Sadiku.

iUniverse books may be ordered through booksellers or by contacting:

iUniverse
1663 Liberty Drive
Bloomington, IN 47403
www.iuniverse.com
844-349-9409

ISBN: 978-1-6632-4118-4 (sc)
ISBN: 978-1-6632-4117-7 (e)

Library of Congress Control Number: 2022911189

Print information available on the last page.

iUniverse rev. date: 06/23/2022

Dedication:

To my daughter

Ann O. Sadiku

CONTENTS

One may regard the whole history of computer science as a record of continuous attempts to discover, study, and implement computing ideas. Computing technology greatly affects nearly every aspect of our modern life including education, entertainment, transportation, communication, economy, medicine, engineering, and science. The history of computing is one of punctuated equilibrium, bringing new and unexpected changes. Mainframes gave birth to minicomputers, which gave birth to workstations, which gave birth to personal computers, which gave birth to smartphones. Modern scientific computing is approaching the point where novel computational algorithms will become indispensable tools.

Although computation was present long before computers were invented, the realization occurred only in the last decade. By the 1980s, computation became so important that it was utterly indispensable in several fields. Computation has become a third leg of science, joining theory and experiment. Thus, computing has been evolving gradually and is now regarded as science. The computer is the tool, while computation is the principle.

We are in the era of computing. Computing is experiencing its most exciting moments in history, permeating nearly all areas of human activities. Computing is any activity that involves using computers. It is any goal-oriented activity requiring the use of computers. It includes designing and building hardware and software systems for a wide range of purposes. It has resulted in deep changes in infrastructures and development practices of computing. It is a critically important, integral component of modern life.

Advancement in technology has led to several computing schemes such as cloud computing, grid computing, green computing, DNA computing, self-aware computing, global computing, etc. No single book can comprehensively cover the breadth of computing technologies available to the scientists and engineers. To the best of the author's knowledge, this is the first time a book will cover all these computing techniques. As far as the author is aware, there are more than 140 computing techniques and this book (in volumes 1 to 3) covers the most important 70 of them. Each chapter acts as a tutorial that introduces readers to an important aspect of computing. The book is more or less an encyclopedia on computing. It covers both the old and the emerging types of computing. The old techniques provide useful information for the new techniques.

The book is divided into three volumes to cover all the topics. This is the second volume with 24 chapters. It covers scientific computing techniques such as natural computing, neural computing, DNA computing, soft computing, organic computing, and stochastic computer, evolutionary computing, biomolecular computing, chemical computing, nano computing, membrane computing, soft computing, autonomic computing, organic computing, location-aware computing, context-aware computing, amorphous computing, symbolic computing, internet computing, and chao computing.

The book is a friendly introduction to various computing techniques. The presentation is clear, succinct, and informal, without proofs or rigorous definitions. The book provides researchers, students, and professionals a comprehensive introduction, applications, benefits, and challenges for each computing technology. The author was motivated to write this book partly due to the lack of a single source of reference on these technologies. There are monographs on some of them, but there is none that combines the computing technologies. Hence, the book will help a beginner to have an introductory knowledge about these technologies. The main objective of the author is to provide a concise treatment that is easily digestible for each computing scheme. It is hoped that the book will be useful to practicing engineers, computer scientists, and information business managers.

I would like to thank the myriad of people who made this work possible. I am grateful to Dr. Pamela Obiomon, dean of the College of Engineering at Prairie View A&M University, and Dr. Kelvin Kirby, head of the Department of Electrical and Computer Engineering for their constant support and appreciation. I would like to thank Dr. Sarhan Musa, Dr. Sudarshan Nelatury, Dr. Mahamadou Temberly, Dr. Emmanual Shadare, and Adedamola Omotoso for their contributions. A well-deserved gratitude goes to my wife Janet for her constant support and prayer.

–Matthew N. O. Sadiku, Prairie View, Texas

1

CHAPTER

NATURAL COMPUTING

People avoid change until the pain of remaining the same is greater than the pain of changing.
- Anonymous

1.1 INTRODUCTION

Although computation was present long before computers were invented, the realization occurred only in the last decade. By the 1980s, computation became so important that it was utterly indispensable in several fields. Computation has become a third leg of science, joining theory and experiment. Thus, computing has been evolving gradually and is now regarded as science [1]. The computer is the tool, while computation is the principle.

Nature has been a dominating component of the world around. Natural computing (or natural computation) refers to the field that deals with computational techniques that take inspiration from nature. It is based on the premise that "nature computes." The multidisciplinary and interdisciplinary aspects of natural computing are illustrated in Figure 1.1 [2]. Due of its interdisciplinary nature, natural computing covers a spectrum of research areas including biology, chemistry, physics, computer science, and engineering. The "classical" nature-inspired models of computation are cellular automata, neural computation, and evolutionary computation. Natural computing includes evolutionary algorithms, artificial neural networks, molecular computing, swarm computing, membrane computing, amorphous computing, cellular computing, nano-computing, quantum computing, and biomolecular (DNA, RNA) computing. These algorithms are commonly grouped together under the names of soft or natural computing. A common characteristic shared by most natural computing algorithms is that they allow learning from data [3]. It has been rightly suggested that the whole universe is a quantum computer that computes its own behavior. When regarded as computations, the processes of nature may be better explained and better understood.

This chapter provides a brief introduction to natural computing (NC). It begins with the fundamentals of NC and then covers its components. It discusses some of the applications of NC. The benefits and challenges of bio-inspired natural computing techniques are discussed. The last section concludes the chapter.

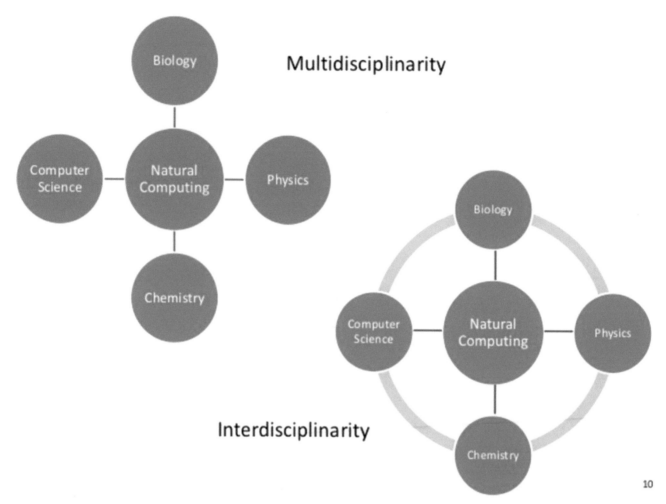

Figure 1.1 Illustration of the multidisciplinary and interdisciplinary aspects of natural computing [2].

1.2 FUNDAMENTALS

Originally, natural computing (NC) contains only biological analogs. Now natural computing contains other nature properties such as physical and chemical. As shown in Figure 1.2, natural computing has many branches. It can be divided into three main branches [4,5]:

1. *Computing inspired by nature*: The key idea here is to develop algorithms by taking inspiration from nature for the solution of complex problems.
2. *The simulation and emulation of nature by means of computing*: This is basically a synthetic process aimed at creating patterns, forms, behaviors, and organisms that resemble "life-as-we-know-it."
3. *Computing with natural materials*: This corresponds to the use of novel natural materials to perform computation.

These three main areas clearly show that knowledge from different research areas are required for a better understanding of life. This requires that physicists, biologists, chemists, engineers, and computer scientists all work together in order to make natural computing feasible. Natural computing algorithms (or nature inspired algorithms) have established their ability to solve a large number of real-world complex problems by providing optimal solutions within the reasonable time duration [6].

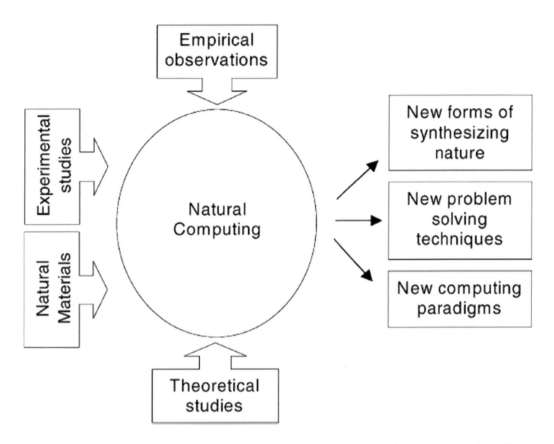

Figure 1.2 Approaches used in developing natural computing and its main branches [4].

1.3 COMPONENTS

Among the many approaches within computing inspired by nature, the most well-known ones are the artificial neural networks, evolutionary algorithms, and swarm intelligence

- *Artificial Neural Networks:* The idea of artificial neural networks (ANNs) was inspired by the structure of the human brain and by envy of what the brain is capable of doing. Although human beings compare poorly to the simplest calculator when it comes to multiplying ten–digit numbers, we are so much better at recognizing the face of a person, the sound of a voice, or the smell of an odor. The most significant characteristic of neural networks is their capability to learn [7]. ANN has the advantage of using well-known characteristics of wavelet and sigmoidal activation function.
- *Evolutionary Computing*: This is also called evolutionary computation. It is the field of research that draws ideas from evolutionary biology. It is inspired by Darwinian evolution of species. Evolutionary computing techniques are efficient, nature-inspired planning and optimization methods based on the principles of natural evolution and genetics. These techniques can be used in problem solving, optimization, and machine learning [8].
- *Swarm Intelligence*: This is inspired by the behavior of groups of organisms. Recent studies have shown that individual social insects such as ants or bees follow simple rules and have no

3

centralized control. The collective behavior of the swarm presents an intelligence that is beyond the intelligence of each individual member [9].

1.4 APPLICATIONS

Research on natural computing has produced several fruits for science, industry, and commerce. Several NC models have been successfully applied to the solution of complex problems related to signal processing, finance, data visualization, data mining, management science, bioinformatics, finance, marketing, engineering, architecture, and design.

- *Finance:* Applications of natural computing in finance include forecasting financial time series, portfolio selection and management, estimating econometric parameters, pricing options, and developing risk management systems, and artificial stock markets [10].
- *Medical Imaging*: Natural computing provides a flexible, application-oriented solutions to current medical image analysis problems, particularly with reference to the applications involving malignancy of the brain, breast, prostate, skin, lung, and liver [11].
- *Bioinformatics:* Natural computing provides several possibilities in bioinformatics. It presents interesting nature-inspired methodologies for handling complex problems such protein structure prediction, microarray data analysis, and gene regulatory network generation [12].

Other common areas of applications of NC include environmental research, disaster monitoring and assessment, modeling of climate/weather, biodiversity analysis and monitoring of wild animals. Python and Julia languages are programming languages used in the specific implementing a natural computing system [13].

1.5 BENEFITS

Bio-inspired natural computing forms the bridge between natural sciences and computer science. It deals with the real world in natural ways. It offers new opportunities to understand, model, and analyze the complexity of the physical world. Natural computing techniques are tools (in hardware, software or wetware) that work better in the natural world where everything is interconnected, nonlinear, and unpredictable. They provide shorter development time, change features easily, and put products into the market quickly and cheaply. They will find their way into appliances, where consumers will expect performance from appliances [14].

1.6 CONCLUSION

Natural computing refers to the field that investigates both human-designed computing inspired by nature and computing taking place in nature. It is a computational version of natural phenomena and processes. It presumes that some form of computation goes on in nature. It is concerned with computational techniques and computational technologies inspired by nature. NC meethods are likely to change the way we do our problem-solving.

For more information on natural computing, one should consult [7,8,15-26] and other books available at Amazon.com. One should also consult the two international journals exclusively devoted to natural computing: *Natural Computing* and *International Journal of Natural Computing Research.*

REFERENCES

[1] P. J. Denning, "Computing is a natural science," *Communication of the ACM,* vol. 50, no. 7, July 2007, pp. 13-18.

[2] L. N. de Castro, "Natural computing - The grand challenges and two case studies," https://www.slideshare.net/lndecastro/2012-natural-computing-the-grand-challenges-and-two-case-studies

[3] K. Worden, W. J. Staszewski, and J. J. Hensman, "Natural computing for mechanical systems research: A tutorial overview," *Mechanical Systems and Signal Processing,* vol. 25, no. 1, Jan. 2011.

[4] "Natural computing," *Wikipedia,* the free encyclopedia https://en.wikipedia.org/wiki/Natural_computing

[5] L. N. de Castro, "Fundamentals of natural computing: An overview," *Physics of Life Reviews,* vol 4, 2017, pp. 1-36.

[6] M. N. O. Sadiku, M. Tembely, and S.M. Musa, "Natural computing," *International Journal of Advanced Research in Computer Science and Software Engineering,* vol. 8, no. 5, May. 2018, pp. 7-9.

[7] M. Giacobibi et al., *Applications of Evolutionary Computing.* Berlin, Germany: Springer-Verlag, 2009.

[8] A. Brabazon and M. O'Neill (eds.), *Natural Computing in Computational Finance.* Berlin, Germany: Springer-Verlag, 2008.

[9] M. N. O. Sadiku and M. Mazzara, "Computing with neural networks," *IEEE Potentials,* October 1993, pp. 14-16.

[10] A. Saggu1, P. Yadav, and M. Roopak, "Applications of swarm intelligence," *International Journal of Computer Science and Mobile Computing,* vol. 2, no. 5, May 2013, pp. 353-359.

[11] S. Mitra and B. U. Shankar, "Medical image analysis for cancer management in natural computing framework," *Information Sciences,* vol. 306, 2015, pp. 111–131.

[12] F. Masulli and S. Mitra, "Natural computing methods in bioinformatics: A survey," *Information Fusion,* vol. 10, 2009, pp. 211–216.

[13] I. Dogaru and R. Dogaru, "Using Python and Julia for efficient implementation of natural computing and complexity related algorithms," *Proceedings of the 20th International Conference on Control Systems and Science,* 2015, pp. 599-604.

[14] J. Huffman, "Natural computing is in your future," *Appliance Manufacturer,* vol. 42, no. 2, Feb. 1994.

[15] L. N. de Castro, *Fundamentals of Natural Computing: Basic Concepts, Algorithms, and Applications.* Boca Raton, FL: CRC Press, 2007.

[16] G. Rozenbera, T. Back, and J. N. Kok (eds), *Handbook of Natural Computing.* Spinger, 4 volumes, 2014.

[17] D. E. Shasha and C. Lazere, *Natural Computing: DNA, Quantum Bits, and the Future of Smart Machines.* New York: W. W. Norton & Company, 2010.

[18] D. H. Ballard, *An Introduction to Natural Computation.* Cambridge, MA: MIT Press, 1999.

[19] J. K. Mandal. S. Mukhopadhyay and T. Pal (eds.), *Handbook of Research on Natural Computing for Optimization Problems*. IGI Global, 2016.

[20] A. Brabazon, M. O'Neil, and S. McGarraghy, *Natural Computing Algorithms*. Springer, 2015.

[21] C. Martín-Vide, R. Neruda, and M. A. Vega-Rodríguez, *Theory and Practice of Natural Computing*. Springer, 2017.

[22] Y. Suzuki and M. Hagiya (eds.), *Recent Advances in Natural Computing*. Springer, 2016.

[23] C. Graciani et al. (eds.), *Enjoying Natural Computing: Essays Dedicated to Mario de Jesús Pérez-Jiménez on the Occasion of His 70th Birthday*. Springer, 2018.

[24] L. N. de Castro, *Natural Computing for Simulation and Knowledge Discovery*. IGI Global, 2013.

[25] X. Li and K. C. Wong (eds.), *Natural Computing for Unsupervised Learning*. Springer, 2018.

[26] W. Brauer et al. (eds.). *Formal and Natural Computing : Essays Dedicated to Grzegorz Rozenberg*. Springer, 2002.

2
CHAPTER

NEURAL COMPUTING

Fame is fleeting.
Money takes wing.
Popularity is an accident.
The only thing that remains is character.
– Anonymous

2.1 INTRODUCTION

Neural computing is a research discipline based on the overlap of brain research and computation. It is a style of computation that draws inspiration from the way the brain computes. It uses computational neural networks (also known as artificial neural networks or neural systems) to perform complex tasks. It is can carry out tasks conventional computers find very difficult. Some have regarded neural computing as a computing alternative in the post-Moore's law era.

The 1980s witnessed a resurgence of interest in neutral networks and neural computing. This new interest is due to the development of new network topologies and algorithms, VLSI implementations as well as by a growing fascination with the functioning of the human brain. This interest is prompted by two facts. First, the nervous system of simple animals can easily solve problems that are very difficult for conventional computers. Such problems include machine or computer vision, pattern recognition, speech recognition, signal processing in the presence of noise and uncertainty, and adaptive learning. Second, the ability to model biological nervous system functions using man-made machines increases understanding of that biological function [1].

This chapter provides an introduction to neural computing. It begins with the fundamentals of neural computing. It discusses some popular neural networks. It provides some applications of neural networks. The last section concludes with some comments.

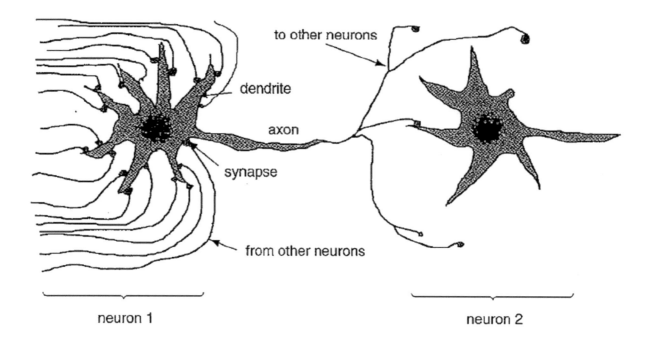

Figure 2.1 – Sketch of typical neurons in human brain [3].

2.2 FUNDAMENTALS

Neural computing (or neuro computing) is information processing implemented by network of neurons. A neuron consists of a cell body, dendrites for receiving inputs, and an axon that transmits the neuron's output to the dendrites of other neurons [2], as shown in Figure 2.1 [3]. Neurons should be regarded as information processing cells. A living neuron usually maintains a voltage drop across its membrane.

Neural computing is the science that deals with a form of computation based on non-programmable processing systems known as neural networks. It is concerned with a class of computing structures that are brain-like in the sense that they acquire knowledge through experience rather than preprogramming.

The idea of neural networks was inspired by the structure of the human brain and by envy of what the brain is capable of doing. Although human beings compare poorly to the simplest calculator when it comes to multiplying ten-digit numbers, we are so much better at recognizing the face of a person, the sound of a voice, or the smell of an odor. We are good at quickly recalling associated facts or past events in our lives. When confronted with new situations, we learn how to fit these situations into our existing knowledge harmoniously.

The most significant characteristic of neural networks is their capability to learn. They familiarize with problems by means of training. After sufficient training, they can solve unknown problems of the same class. There is no need to explicitly program a neural network. For instance, it can learn from training samples or by means of encouragement [4].

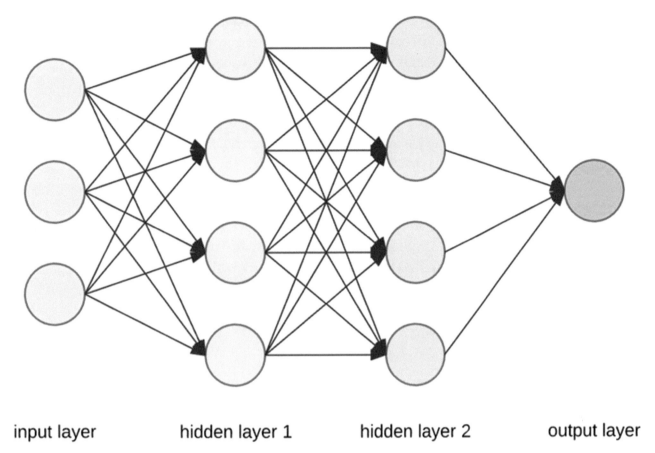

input layer   hidden layer 1   hidden layer 2   output layer

Figure 2.2 A typical neural network [7].

2.3 NEURAL NETWORKS

Neural computing is basically computing with neural networks. These networks have been studied extensively with the hope of achieving human-like performance in the fields of speech and image recognition. Work on neural network has been inspired by knowledge of neural computation. A neural network is basically a complex, mathematical equation that works with numbers. The network takes some data in and produces another data as results [5].

A neural network is essentially an interconnected assembly of simple processing elements or nodes, which are the artificial equivalents of biological neurons. The processing ability of the network is stored in the interelement connection strengths or weights, obtained by a process of learning [6]. Network topology depicts the way neurons are interconnected. It varies from fully-connected to multi-layered networks. A typical neural network is shown in Figure 2.2 [7].

There are different types of neural networks. The most popular neural network types are artificial neural networks (ANN), multilayer perceptrons (MLP, and self-organizing maps (MOPs). Here we consider these three well-known neural networks.

- *Artificial Neural Networks* (ANN): One of popular neural computing models is the ANN, which is a simulation environment based on structure of biological neural system. ANN has attracted particular attention due to its ability to learn from past experience. Typically, it consists of one input layer and one output layer and may have one or more hidden layers. ANNs can model nonlinear processes with few a priori assumptions about the nature of the underlying process [8].

- *Self-organizing Maps* (SOMs): These are a neural computing paradigm that identifies orthogonal clusters within a dataset. They have been used in engineering, climate science research, medical research, geographic information sciences, and the environmental sciences [9].
- *Multilayer Perceptron* (MLP): This typically consists of a set of source units that constitute the input layer, one or more hidden layers of neurons and an output layer

A key feature of neural networks is an iterative learning process presented to the network one at a time. The learning algorithm is a procedure that adjusts the weights connecting the nodes in order to minimize the difference between the output and the target. Backpropagation is the most popular method for training multilayer feed forward networks and is the most popular learning algorithm. The goal of backpropagation algorithm is to teach the network to associate specific output to each of several inputs.

Deep-learning network is the name given to a network composed of several layers. It is distinguished from the more commonplace single-hidden-layer neural network by its depth, which is the number of node layers through which data must pass.

2.4 APPLICATIONS

Since neural systems attempt to reflect cognitive processes and behavior, the field is closely related to cognitive and behavioral modeling. Neural computing is a rapidly expanding area of current research, attracting researchers from a wide variety of disciplines. It unites a broad range of experts such as engineers, physicists, statisticians, parallel processing experts, optical technologists, and experimental biologists. It is successfully applied in various fields such as pattern classification, image processing, data recovery, image processing and optimization problems, pharmaceutical product development, target marketing, production systems, forecasting and modeling, speech, robotics, finance, civil engineering, power systems. control systems, and other scientific disciplines.

For the purpose of illustration, we will provide more information on three of these applications.

- *Chemical science*: Neural computing is a powerful tool for developing accurate models for chemical phenomena. A wide range of problems in chemistry have enjoyed the flexibility and power that is offered by neural computing. Applications include predicting chemical reactivity, protein structure determination, process control, pattern recognition and matching, structural identification, and data analysis [10].
- *Medical Imaging*: The use of neural computing techniques in medical imaging is now very widespread. Computer-aided medical diagnosis has become an important interdisciplinary technology, yielding non-invasive accurate diagnoses [11].
- *Power systems*: Neural networks are more suited than conventional techniques in solving complex problems in power systems. For example, security assessment of power systems is difficult with conventional approaches. A neural network can be trained using a set of data obtained from off-line analysis of the power network. After training, the approximate solution obtained is judged adequate for assessing the security of the power system [12].
- *Business:* Neural computing is being adopted world wide to provide decision support for a wide variety of business problems. Applications of neural computing to business problems include bank failure prediction, firm bankruptcy prediction, loan application approval, predicting rating of corporate bonds, fraud prevention, data validation, risk management, predicting rating of corporate

bonds, fraud prevention, online credit scoring, profiling customers, behavioral monitoring, and database marketing [13].

- *Virtual Reality:* Virtual reality is a new display technology or computer user interface for providing users with real viewing experience. Virtual reality technology has been developed based on some core technologies including computer graphics, image processing, simulations, human–computer interfaces, and sensors. Neural computing technology is expected to be one of the technologies of virtual reality [14].

2.5 BENEFITS

Conventional-sequential computers are usually programmed to solve a given problem. Neural computers follow an alternative approach in that they are inspired by the human brain. They learn from experience and can extract essential characteristics from noisy data. They are ideally suited for real-world applications by providing solutions for hard problems. Some applications take advantage of the nature parallelism of neural networks. They can be applied in the formulation of problems with a comparable with that of statistics. They can classify patterns on which they have not been trained.

Other main benefits of neural computing include [5]:

- *Programmability:* The main advantage of a neural network is its programmability. Because neural networks learn from the data given to them, they are very versatile.
- *Accuracy*: By learning from experience and not through programming, the systems can provide recommendations on tough decisions.
- *Speed:* Neural networks can potentially operate at considerable speeds.

2.6 CONCLUSION

Neural computing involves computing with neural networks. These networks can store experiential knowledge, which is acquired through training rather than programming. It is leading to breakthroughs in applications such as signal processing, pattern recognition, and optimization.

For more information on neural computing, one should consult the books on it [6, 15-21] and other books available on Amazon.com. One should also consult the following journals devoted to it:

- *Neural Networks*
- *International Journal of Neural Systems*
- *Neural Computation*
- *Neurocomputing*
- *IEEE Transactions on Neural Networks and Learning Systems*
- *Neural Computing and Applications*
- *Neural Processing Letters*

REFERENCES

[1]   M. N. O. Sadiku and M. Mazzara, "Computing with neural networks," *IEEE Potentials,* October 1993, pp. 14-16.

[2]   P. Treleaven and M. Vellasco, "Neural computing overview," *Computer Physics Communications,* vol. 57, 1989, pp. 543-559.

[3]   R. Aggarwal and Y. Song, "Artificial neural networks in power systems: Part I General introduction to neural computing," *Power Engineering,* June 1997, pp. 129-134.

[4]   D. Kriesel, "A brief introduction to neural networks," http://www.dkriesel.com/en/science/neural_networks

[5]   G. Bolt, "Neural computing – What it will and will not do," *Credit Control,* vol. 23, 3, 2002, pp. 13-17.

[6]   K. Gurney, *An Introduction to Neural Networks.* London, UK: UCL Press, 1997.

[7]   K. Sorokina, "Image classification with convolutional neural networks," Nov. 2017, https://medium.com/@ksusorokina/image-classification-with-convolutional-neural-networks-496815db12a8

[8]   J. Zahavi and N. Levin, "Applying neural computing to target marketing," *Journal of Direct Marketing,* vol. 11, no. 4, Fall 1997, pp. 75-93.

[9]   M. J. Somers and J. Casal, "Introducing neural computing in governance research: Applying Sself-organizing maps to configurational studies," *Corporate Governance: An International Review,* vol. 25, 2017, pp. 440–453.

[10]   B. G. Sumpter, C. Getino, and D. W. Noid, "Theory and applications of neural computation in chemical science," *Annual Review of Physical Chemistry,* vol. 45, 1994. pp. 439-481.

[11]   F. Gorunescu et al., "Competitive/collaborative neural computing system for medical diagnosis in pancreatic cancer detection," *Expert Systems,* vol. 28, no. 1, Feb. 2011, pp. 33-48.

[12]   B. H. Chowdhury and B. M. Wilamoski, "Security assessment using neural computing" *Proceedings of the First International Forum o Applications of Neural Networks to Power Systems,* July 1991.

[13]   J. Zahavi and N. Levin, "Applying neural computing to target marketing," *Journal of Direct Marketing,* vol. 11. no. 1, Winter 1997, pp. 5-22.

[14]   Z. Lv, J. J. Wang, and X. Luo, "Editorial: neural computing in next-generation virtual reality technology," *Neural Computing and Applications,* vol. 29, 2018, pp. 1195–1198.

[15]   L. Tarassenko, *A Guide to Neural Computing Applications.* John Wiley & Sons, 1998.

[16]   R. Beale and T. Jackson, *Neural Computing - An Introduction.* Boca Raton, FL: CRC Press,1990.

[17]   L. Taraseenko, *A Guide to Neural Computing Applications.* New York: John Wiley & Sons, 1998.

[18]   S. K. Pal, L. Polkowski, and A. Skowron (eds.), *Rough-Neural Computing: Techniques for Computing with Words.* Springer, 2004.

[19]   G. Deco and D. Obradovic, *An Information-Theoretic Approach to Neural Computing.* Springer, 1996.

[20]   I. Aleksander, *Neural Computing Architectures: The Design of Brain-Like Machines.* MIT Press, 1989.

[21]   A. J. Maren, C. T. Harston, and R. M. Pap, *Handbook of Neural Computing Applications.* San Diego, CA: Academic Press, 1990.

3

RESERVOIR COMPUTING

The 12 principles of character: (1) Honesty,
(2) Understanding, (3) Compassion,
(4) Appreciation, (5) Patience, (6) Discipline,
(7) Fortitude, (8) Perseverance, (9) Humor,
(10) Humility, (11) Generosity, (12) Respect.
- Kathryn B. Johnson

3.1 INTRODUCTION

Reservoir computing (RC) is an umbrella term for a number of different machine learning techniques that use the high-dimensional transient dynamics of an excitable system, also called the "reservoir." It is a powerful machine learning technique for temporal information processing [1]. It may be regarded as a neuromorphic computing scheme inspired by the human brain. It is a highly efficient bio-inspired approach suited for processing time-dependent information. In principle, any dynamical system with rich dynamics can be used to build a reservoir.

Reservoir computing is a relatively new concept in the field of neural networks and machine learning. It has emerged recently in response to demands for increasingly complex real-time signal processing methods based on new technologies. Reservoir computers are a subset of neural networks that behave as a dynamical system rather than a function. It represents an alternative recurrent neural network model that provides fast training. It may be regarded as a novel, promising approach for processing temporal data or a method of efficiently training recurrent neural networks to perform a given task.

This chapter provides a primer on reservoir computing. It begins by discussing the concept and implementations of reservoir computing. Then it covers some applications, benefits, and challenges of reservoir computing. The last section closes with remarks.

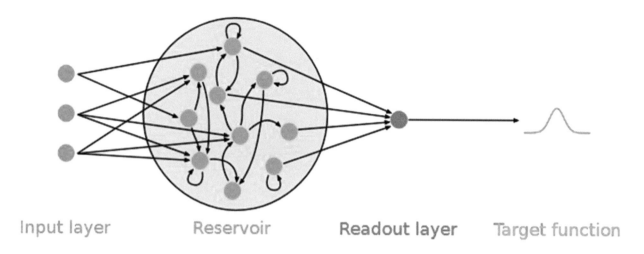

Input layer   Reservoir   Readout layer   Target function

Figure 3.1 The reservoir computing architecture [3].

3.2 CONCEPT OF RESERVOIR COMPUTING

Reservoir computing (RC) is essentially a recent trend in neural networks. It is a new computing paradigm that allows harnessing the dynamics of a reservoir (or compute core) to perform computations. RC is a new training concept for recurrent neural networks. It came from machine learning and neural networks. It initially emerged as a software-only technique and used as an algorithmic way of processing temporal data. It has been successfully used in pattern classification problems such as like speech and image recognition and time series prediction [2].

The concept of reservoir computing was conceived in 2001 by Herbert Jaeger and Wolfgang Maass while working independently. It originated from a pioneering study on echo state networks and liquid state machines in the early 2000s, The RC concept was first introduced using an recurrent neural network (RNN) as a reservoir. The reservoir computing architecture is shown in Figure 3.1 [3]. RC divides the RNN into two components: the untrained recurrent part (a reservoir) and the trainable feed-forward part (a readout layer). The reservoir is a dynamical system that can respond to inputs and is used to postprocess the signal from sensing elements that are placed separately. The readout layer that is used to analyze the state of the system. In principle, any complex dynamical system equipped with a readout layer can be used for any computation by only adjusting the readout layer. Thus the RC paradigm is flexible and relatively straight forward to implement [4].

The RC differs from traditional feed-forward neural networks by the following characteristics [5]:

- The network nodes each have distinct dynamical behavior
- Time delays of signals may occur along the network links
- The network's hidden part has recurrent connections
- The input and internal weights are fixed and chosen randomly
- Only the output weights are adjusted during training.

RC systems are commonly used with analog or binary neurons in the recurrent circuits. The reservoir consists of a collection of recurrently connected units. It is generated randomly and only the output layer needs training. The overall dynamics of the reservoir are driven by the input, and also affected by the past. Like a conventional neural network, a reservoir consists of a large number of interconnected nonlinear nodes [6]. The large number of nonlinear nodes makes RC capable of solving complex tasks. Due to its simplicity and flexibility, RC is amenable to a large number of implementations. RC can be implemented using any physical system that offers enough dynamics for information processing, provided the three commonly cited sufficient conditions for RC are met: separation of input states, generalization of similar inputs to similar outputs, and fading memory [7].

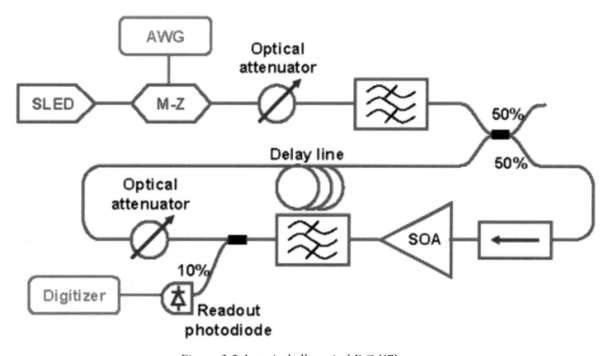

Figure 3.2 A typical all-optical RC [17].

3.3 IMPLEMENTATIONS

RC mimics human-like computational power and is made of a simple structure. Different types of reservoir computers have been developed. Some are derived from several recurrent neural networks (RNNs). The two most common approaches in Reservoir Computing are known as Echo State Network (ESN) proposed by Herbert Jaeger and asynchronous Liquid State Machine (LSM) introduced by Wolfgang Maas [8].

- *Echo State Network* (ESN) consists of a random, recurrent network of neurons that is driven by a time signal, and the activations of the neurons are used to do linear classification/regression. The ESN was introduced by Jaeger and his team as a better way to use the computational power of RNNs without the hassle of training the internal weights [9]. ESN was described as a constructive learning algorithm for recurrent neural networks. It has been successfully applied to many engineering problems such as chaotic time series forecasting, mainly due to their speed of training and avoidance of many common shortcomings of typical RNNs.

- *Liquid State Machine* (LSM): This approach has close links to the Echo State Network although these two theories have been independently developed. LSM was originally presented as a general framework to perform real-time computation on temporal signals. It was introduced by Maass.

LSM has become more popular in computational neuroscience field. In robotics, LSMs have been used to control a simulated robot arm and model an existing robot controller [9].

Both and a few other methods are subsumed under the more general term reservoir computing. Several variants of RC models have been proposed to improve the performance of the conventional ones. Since most implementations of RC have been software based, and thereby they are limited in speed and power efficiency. Efficient hardware implementations are highly desired. A dedicated hardware implementation can offer an advantage over software implementations. Hardware implementations of RC have been done in electronics, optics, and optoelectronics [10].

- *Electronic RC*: RC systems implemented with electronic circuits and devices have been actively studied for developing machine learning devices with low training cost. They reduce energy consumption, speed up computation, and cope with imperfection and noise in hardware. Implementations of RC using real-time field programmable gate array (FPGA) have been studied [11].
- *Memristive RC:* Different physical devices have been used to form reservoirs, including memristors and photonics. A network of memristors can be used as a reservoir to nonlinearly map an input signal into a high-dimensional feature space. The memristor is a nanoscale device that exhibits an inherent memory property, i.e., its current state depends on the past. Environment sensitive memristors have successfully been used to build efficient reservoir computers. Memristive components serve as reservoir building blocks that are assembled into device networks. Memcapacitors offer great promise for power-efficient reservoir computers [12]. Even a small hardware system with only 88 memristors can be used for tasks, such as handwritten digit recognition [13].
- *Photonic RC:* Photonics-based reservoir computers are at the forefront of RC technologies. The remarkable speed and multiplexing capability of optics makes it very attractive for information processing. Light-based (photonic) technologies offer some benefits when it comes to building a computer: they are efficient, have high bandwidths, deliver fast processing speeds, and are immune to electromagnetic interference [14]. Because of these benefits, photonic RC has some advantages over the other implementations and is widely used in telecommunications. Photonics seems to be a good candidate of building a reservoir since it offers the potential for a fast, power efficient, and massively parallel hardware implementation. Photonic cavities on chip is the ideal candidate for an optical reservoir computer. Such a photonic implementation offers the promise of low power consumption and the high processing speeds. The photonic reservoir can be used in pattern recognition tasks such as header recognition [15]. It can successfully perform a variety of tasks such as bit level tasks and non-linear dispersion compensation at high speeds and low power consumption [16].
- *All-Optical RC:* All-optical computing RC with state-of-the-art performance is possible. The all-optical reservoir is implemented using off-the-shelf fiber components operating in the C-band. The system design is based on a optical delayed feedback loop combined to the nonlinearity of an optical amplifier. It could be made of off-the-shelf components for optical telecommunications. Such reservoir computing is highly flexible. A typical all-optical RC is shown in Figure 3.2 [17].

Other implementations include mechanical RC, spintronic RC, and biological RC.

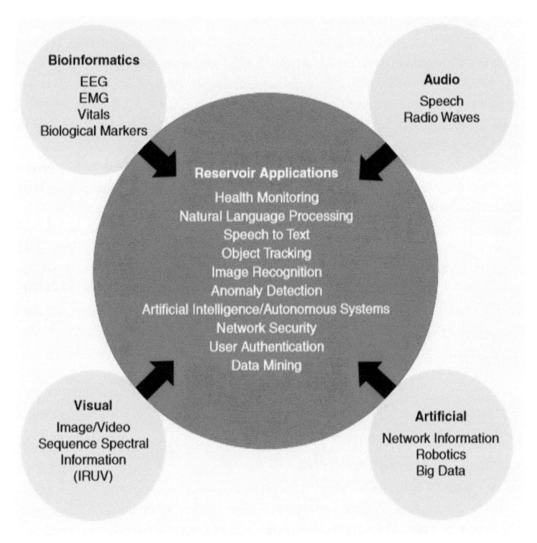

Figure 3.3 Some applications of reservoir computing [18].

3.4 APPLICATIONS

Due to the inherent flexibility of implementation, new applications of RC are being reported constantly. These include robotics, embedded systems, sensing applications, digital signal processing, human action recognition, financial forecasting, bio-medical applications, weather or stock market prediction, self-driven cars, speech processing, pattern recognition, NLP, computational neuroscience, machine learning, and language interpretation. For some of these applications, RC is the most powerful approach known at present.

A goal of reservoir computing is to develop techniques that can solve real world problems. However, many of the applications so far involve temporal/sequential data processing. Some of these applications are shown in Figure 3.3 [18]. The following applications are just typical [19,20]:

- *Speech Recognition:* Speech recognition is an obvious application of reservoir systems. Although speech recognition is a difficult problem, reservoir computing along with classical neural networks has been employed with success.

- *Robotics:* The temporal nature of reservoir models also makes them suitable for robotic systems which process sensor data over time. Deadbeat controllers can be obtained through a careful training of Echo State Networks. RC is used for detecting complex events in autonomous robot navigation. It is well suited to solve some robot-related problems such as learning by example, robot localization, map and path generation.
- *Financial Forecasting:* The global markets constitute one of the most complex systems in modern society. Financial forecasting is a non-trivial engineering task. There has been a growing need for intelligent systems for forecasting dynamics and future directions of global economy. An accurate prediction of the future enables companies and governments in planning. Artificial neural networks are trainable systems that have powerful learning capabilities with application in financial forecasting. Forecasting is complex and difficult as the stock market is the result of interactions of many variables and players. The ability of the echo state network to learn chaotic time series makes it a useful tool for financial forecasting where data is very nonlinear and complex [21].
- *Medical Systems:* Since neural networks are modeled after biological systems, one of the obvious applications is to see how they mimic biological or medical systems.
- *Music:* Reservoirs have been trained to hum a melody and re-create a cyclical temporal pattern.

3.5 BENEFITS

RC offers some advantages over other methods for classifying and forecasting time-series data. RC with classical neural networks has been applied with success to a variety of complex speech recognition and classification problems. It has been shown to have the potential to model complex, nonlinear dynamic systems. It can also be applied to time-independent signals such as images. RC has been employed successfully in several complex machine learning tasks such as dynamic pattern recognition, chaotic time series recognition, speech recognition, time-series prediction, classification problem, and noise modelling [22]. Reservoir computing offers an intuitive means of using temporal processing power of recurrent neural networks (RNNs) without the need of training them.

RC is a versatile and flexible concept. Because of this flexibility, reservoir computing is amenable to a large number of experimental implementations. RC has emerged as a promising technique for exploiting physical systems directly as computing substrates, where the computation happens "for free" in the rich physical domain. One advantage of RC is to use a fixed randomly connected network as reservoir, without training burden.

Another major benefit of RC is its ability to use the transient dynamics of a physical system for information processing. The relatively low cost of training RC models due to fast learning ability is an appealing advantage over more traditional RNNs. Another advantage is that the reservoir without adaptive updating is amenable to hardware implementation using a variety of physical systems [23]. Reservoir computing networks can play the role of a universal dynamical system capable of learning the dynamics of other systems. The networks can identify and generalize linear and non-linear transformations and serve as robust and effective image classifiers.

3.6 CHALLENGES

Although researchers have applied reservoir computing successfully to a variety of problems, there are still many open questions that need to be addressed. One shortcoming of the RC algorithm is that the models will not perform well without sufficient large training sets. Unlike the traditional computation models, RC is a dynamical system in which computation and memory are inseparable, and therefore hard to analyze. Having a fully implemented reservoir computer with a high number of nodes remains a technological challenge. Delay is omnipresent, in almost every system, especially biological systems.

3.7 CONCLUSION

Reservoir computing is a recurrent neural network scheme that is becoming popular due to its simplicity and superior performance on a number of time-series prediction and classification problems. It is specifically designed for processing time-dependent data. It can serve as a universal system capable of learning the dynamics of other systems.

Interest in RC has grown over recent years in three main research areas: (1) neuroscience and cognitive science, (2) machine learning, and (3) unconventional computing [1]. It has attracted interest in a broad range of research fields, not just only in the machine-learning or neural networks community but also in mathematics, physics, chemistry, engineering, computer science, nanotechnology, and robotics. Experts in these fields should work hand in hand to develop the concept and explore applications. More information about RC can be found in the books in [24-25].

REFERENCES

[1]   A. Goudarzi and C. Teuscher, "Reservoir computing: Quo Vadis?" *NanoCom'16*, New York, September 203.

[2]   M. N. O. Sadiku, K. G. Eze, and S. M. Musa, "Reservoir computing," *International Journal of Trend in Research and Development*, vol. 5, no. 6, November-December 2018, pp.17-18.

[3]   J. H. Jensen and G. Tufte, "Reservoir computing with a chaotic circuit," *Proceedings of ECAL 2017: The Fourteenth European Conference on Artificial Life*, September 2017, pp. 222-229.

[4]   Z. Konkoli, "On developing theory of reservoir computing for sensing applications: the state weaving environment echo tracker (SWEET) algorithm," *International Journal of Parallel, Emergent and Distributed Systems*, vol. 33, no. 2, 2108, pp. 121-143.

[5]   D. J. Gauthier, "Reservoir computing: Harnessing a universal dynamical system," *SIAM News*, March 2018, p. 12.

[6]   G. Van der Sande, D. Brunner, and M. C. Soriano, "Advances in photonic reservoir computing," *Nanophotonics*, vol. 6, no. 3, 2017, pp. 561–576.

[7]   N. D. Haynes et al., "Reservoir computing with a single time-delay autonomous Boolean node," *Physical Review*, vol. E 91, 2015.

[8]   K. Stanek, "Reservoir computing in financial forecasting with committee methods," *Master's Thesis*, Technical University of Denmar, 2011.

[9]   *Proceedings of European Symposium on Artificial Neural Networks*, Bruges, Belgium, April 2007, pp. 471-482.

[10]   M. C. Soriano et al., "Delay-based reservoir computing: Noise effects in a combined analog and digital implementation," *IEEE Transactions on Neural Networks and Learning Systems*, vol. 26, no. 2, February 2015, pp. 388-393.

[11]   G. Tanaka et al., "Recent advances in physical reservoir computing: A review," *Neural Networks,* vol.115, July 2019, pp. 100-123.

[12]   S. J. Dat Tran and C. Teuscher, "Memcapacitive reservoir computing," *IEEE/ACM International Symposium on Nanoscale Architectures,* 2017, pp. 115 – 13.

[13]   C. Du et al., "Reservoir computing using dynamic memristors for temporal information processing," *Nature Communications,* vol. 8, December 2017.

[14]   M. C. Soriano, "Reservoir computing speeds up," *Physics,* February 2017.

[15]   F. Laporte1, J. Dambre, and P. Bienstman, "Reservoir computing with signal-mixing cavities," *Proceedings of the 19th International Conference on Transparent Optical Networks,* 2017.

[16]   A. Katumba et al., "Neuromorphic computing based on silicon photonics and reservoir computing," *IEEE Journal of Selected Topics in Quantum Electronics*, vol. 24, no. 6, November/December 2018.

[17]   F. Duport et al., "All-optical reservoir computing," *Optics Express,* vol. 20, no. 20. 2012, pp. 22783-22795.

[18]   N. Soures et al., "Reservoir computing in embedded system," *IEEE Consumer Electronics Magazine,* July 2017, pp. 67-73.

[19]   A. Roli, "Introduction to reservoir computing methods," https://amslaurea.unibo.it/8268/1/melandri_luca_tesi.pdf

[20]   T. E. Gibbons, "Reservoir computing: A rich area for undergraduate research," https://pdfs.semanticscholar.org/eb5f/d07b4deb77a003af1ce234886c1fc6a9dd31.pdf

[21]   J. Su, "Reservoir computing in forecasting financial markets," *Master's Thesis,* Duke University, April 2015.

[22]   M. R. Salehi and L. Dehyadegari, "Optical signal processing using photonic reservoir computing," *Journal of Modern Optics,* vol. 61, no. 17, 2014, pp. 1442-1451.

[23]   G. Tanakaa et al., "Recent advances in physical reservoir computing: A review," *Neural Networks*, vol. 115, 2019, pp. 100–123.

[24]   K. Nakajima and I. Fischer (eds.), *Reservoir Computing Theory, Physical Implementations, and Applications.* Springer, 2020.

[25]   D. Brunner, M. C. Soriano, and G. V. er Sande (eds.), *Photonic Reservoir Computing: Optical Recurrent Neural Networks.* De Gruyter, 2019.

4
CHAPTER

EVOLUTIONARY COMPUTING

The best thing to give your enemy is forgiveness;
to an opponent, tolerance;
to a friend, your heart;
to your child, a good example;
to a father, deference;
to your mother, conduct that will make her proud of you; to yourself, respect;
to all men, charity.
– Arthur J. Balfour

4.1 INTRODUCTION

Evolution has been a source of inspiration for algorithm designers since the invention of the digital computers. The resulting field is evolutionary computation [1]. Evolutionary computation is branch of computer science that applies ideas from biological evolution to solve problems. It mimics the processes of biological evolution with its ideas of natural selection and survival of the fittest to solve optimization problems. It uses algorithms such as genetic algorithms, genetic programming, evolutionary strategies, immune programming, artificial neural network, and evolutionary programming.

Evolutionary computation (EC) is a branch of natural computing that covers a wide range of problem-solving optimization techniques, which are based on principles of biological evolution. By nature, biological systems are asynchronous. Evolution is in essentially a two-step process of random variation and selection.

Evolutionary computing (EC) refers to a range of problem-solving techniques based on principles of biological evolution, such as reproduction, mutation, recombination, natural selection, genetic inheritance, and survival of the fittest. It is a subfield of artificial intelligence (AI) and also an important part of computational intelligence. It is rapidly growing area that involves computer science, mathematics, economics and management, engineering, physical science, and many other fields. It is an exciting discipline that considers evolutionary programming, evolution strategies, genetic algorithms, and genetic programming as sub-fields [2]. It deals with techniques and concepts that are continually and selectively evolving and optimizing. The techniques are used on problems that have too many variables for traditional algorithms. EC techniques can produce highly optimized solutions in a wide range of problem settings. They are being applied with success to a variety of problems, ranging from practical applications in industry to leading-edge scientific research.

This chapter provides an introduction on evolutionary computing. It begins with discussing the main features of EC. Then it addresses EC techniques, applications, advantages and disadvantages. It covers the benefits and challenges of EC. The last section concludes with some comments.

4.2 FEATURES OF EVOLUTIONARY COMPUTING

As the name suggests, evolutionary computation is a special kind of computing, which draws inspiration from the process of evolution. The term "evolutionary computation" was officially coined in 1993 when the academic journal, *Evolutionary Computation,* began its publication at the MIT Press. EC is based on Charles Darwin's notion of an evolutionary system. It has its roots in nature. It is a form of a search algorithm in which principles of natural evolution are regarded as rules for optimization. It involves building, applying, and studying algorithms based on the Darwinian principles of natural selection. It is a population-based optimization method.

Evolutionary computing methods are weak search-and-optimization techniques inspired by natural evolution. They have proven to be effective in a wide range of applications such as feature selection, electrical-circuit synthesis, and data mining [3].

Evolutionary computing involves the process of continuous optimization like the allied field of computational intelligence. It includes a variety of algorithms and problem-solving techniques such as genetic algorithms, genetic programming, evolutionary strategies, immune programming, artificial neural network, evolutionary programming, and a host of others.

The most important components of evolutionary computing approach are [4]:

- Representation (members of the population)
- Evaluation/Objective function (or fitness function)
- Population as a collection of individuals
- Parent selection mechanism
- Variation operators, recombination and mutation
- Survivor selection mechanism (replacement)

Evolutionary computing refers to a set of problem-solving techniques based on the Darwinian principles of natural selection and evolution. Concepts from biology are applied in EC. The concepts include representation, populations, initialization, parents, offspring, selection, recombination, mutation, survival, and termination [5]. An EC starts with a set of individuals which form its population. It is common to randomly generate the initial population. For each iteration, the algorithm evaluates each individual using the fitness function and terminates if it finds acceptable solutions. Otherwise, it selects several individuals to replace individuals in the population that were not selected for reproduction. Then, the algorithm manipulates individuals in the population by applying different evolutionary operators. Individuals from the previous population are called parents; those created by applying evolutionary operators to the parents are called offspring [6]. Survival of the fittest implies that only organisms with a high degree of fitness are retained in a generation for the mutation.

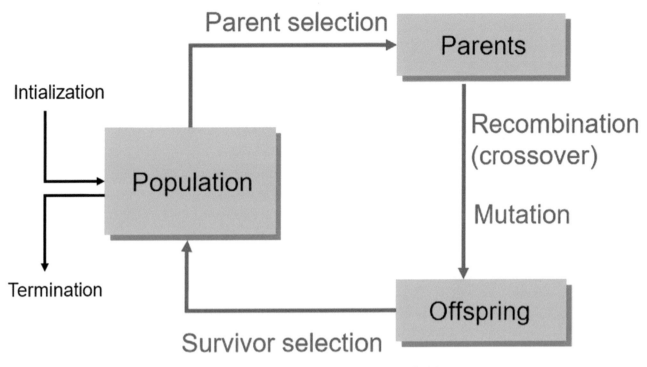

Figure 4.1 The main evolutionary cycle [7].

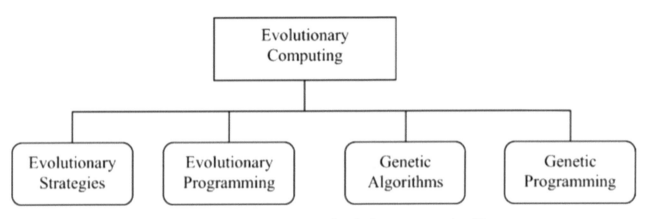

Figure 4.2 Main components of evolutionary computing [8].

4.3 EVOLUTIONARY COMPUTING TECHNIQUES

The main evolutionary paradigms include genetic algorithm, genetic programming, evolution strategies, evolutionary programming, particle swarm optimization, ant colony optimization, differential evolution, and quantum-inspired evolutionary algorithm. Each paradigm uses population-based probabilistic search, a powerful tool for broad exploration and local exploitation. In nature, evolution operates on populations of organisms, natural selection allows the members that serve to be passed on to the next generation, while those that did not die out. EC models the essential elements of biological evolution and explores the solution space by gene inheritance, mutation, and selection of the fittest candidate solutions. The main evolutionary cycle is shown in Figure 4.1 [7]. Evolutionary processes can easily be simulated in a digital computer, where millions of generations can be executed. Evolutionary computing techniques are applied to a wide range of computing problems. Its main components are illustrated in Figure 4.2 [8]. The main difference in the four components is how the new generation is created using the candidates from previous generations.

- *Evolutionary Algorithm* (EA): This is a subset of evolutionary computation. Evolutionary algorithms are used in solving a wide variety of continuous, discrete, and combinatorial optimization problems. EAs usually perform well approximating solution to all types of problems. In most applications of EAs, computational complexity is the major prohibiting factor [9]. An EA often starts with a randomly initialized population. It maintains a population of candidate solutions to a given problem. This population is iteratively refined over time by evolving members of the population. The population of solutions gets updated iteratively using algorithm-specific heuristics until convergence is achieved. The most important components are as follows [10]:
  - representation (definition of individuals)
  - evaluation function (or fitness function)
  - population
  - parent selection mechanism
  - variation operators, recombination and mutation
  - survivor selection mechanism (replacement)

Due to their random nature, EAs never guarantee to provide an optimal solution for any problem, but they will often find a good solution if one exists. EAs have been applied successfully to a wide range of tasks in machine learning and supervised learning.

- *Genetic Algorithm* (GA): This is the most widely used evolutionary computing technique due to its simplicity and flexibility. It was proposed by John Holland in the early 1970s. A GA is a directed random search technique based on mechanics of natural selection and natural genetics. A random population is generated which is then evolved towards better solutions through various iterations known as generations. The algorithm applies the principle of survival of the fittest to produce better and better approximations to a solution. The algorithm is terminated when either the required fitness is achieved or the number of cycles are completed. Otherwise the next generation is created by selecting best candidate from previous generations and so on. GA can be implemented using following steps [11]:

Step-1: Initialize random population

Step-2: Calculate fitness function of each candidate solution

Step-3: Select best-ranking candidates to mate pairs at random

Step-4: Apply crossover operator

Step-5: Calculate fitness function of each candidate solution (optional) apply mutation operator

Step-6: Check whether the terminating condition fulfilled (e.g. desired fitness achieved or enough number of cycles completed). If yes then terminate algorithm otherwise go to step 3

GA has been successfully applied to solve many problems such as mechanical design, electromagnetic optimization, bioinformatics, environmental protection, finance, musical orchestration, and nuclear reactor core design.

- *Evolutionary Programming* (EP): This was originally developed by Fogel, Ownes and Walsh in the mid sixties, when they simulated evolution as a learning process with the aim of generating artificial intelligence. EP is similar to the evolutionary strategies (ES), but it was developed independently. In EP the evolutionary process is focused on the level of whole species not on single individuals.
- *Genetic Programming* (GP): This is basically a special type of genetic algorithm. It uses the principles of genetics and Darwinian natural selection to evolve computer programs. GP is largely related to GA regarding the general processing scheme. But instead of representing attributes in a general binary coding, genetic Programming is specialized on representing instructions.
- *Swarm Intelligence:* Particle swarm optimization (PSO), ant colony optimization, and bee colony optimization are collectively known as swarm intelligence. In PSO, an initial population of candidate solution (called particles) is formed having random position and velocities. PSO has been applied to the localization problem of a mobile robot.

4.4 APPLICATIONS

Evolutionary computing has been successfully applied to several numerical and optimization problems because it has the advantage of giving reasonably acceptable solution in a reasonable amount of time. Its applicability is broad and comprehensive, covering most problems that can be cast as an optimization task. EC can be used as efficient problem solvers for optimization, controls, constraint handling, machine learning, and modeling tasks [12]. A main feature of evolutionary computing is its efficient solution-searching ability in nonlinear optimization problems. EC has also found a vast field of applications in which optimization is not the main concern.

- *Medicine:* The application of evolutionary computation to problems in medicine has increased rapidly, but there are challenges that distinguish it from other real-world applications. Obtaining reliable and coherent patient data, establishing the clinical need and demonstrating value in the results obtained are all aspects that require careful and detailed consideration. For example, medical applications include diagnosis and monitoring of Parkinson's disease, detection of breast cancer from mammograms, and. cancer screening using Raman spectroscopy [13].
- *Business:* Credit has become an important part of our lifestyle as we routinely use credit cards, which are the most popular form of credit. The financial institutions have the challenge of determining applicants that are credit worthy. Evolutionary computing has been used in credit scoring and credit risk management. Credit scoring systems based on evolutionary computation have been tried with some success in terms of predictive power [14]. Evolutionary algorithms have also been used in detecting fraud, which is characterized as an activity that is illegal.
- *Architectural Space Planning:* This is one of the most difficult problem in architectural design. It involves finding of feasible locations for a set of interrelated objects such as rooms, walls, etc. A lot of effort has been made toward the use of evolutionary computing for architectural space planning problem [4].

Other applications include particle filtering, hydrogeological science, groundwater remediation, global optimization, circuit design and layout, spacecraft trajectories, antenna design, recommender systems, weather forecasting, network-on-chip design, petroleum industry, and a host of others.

4.5 ADVANTAGES AND DISADVANGES OF EC

Some of the advantages of evolutionary computing include [7]:

- No presumptions with respect to problem space
- Widely applicable
- Low development and application costs
- Easy to incorporate other methods
- Solutions are interpretable
- Can be run interactively, accommodate user proposed solutions
- Provides many alternative solutions
- Intrinsic parallelism, straightforward parallel implementations

The disadvantages of evolutionary computing include [7]:

- No guarantee for optimal solution within finite time
- Weak theoretical basis
- May need parameter tuning
- Often computationally expensive, i.e. slow

4.6 BENEFITS AND CHALLENGES

Specific benefits of using EC over classic methods of optimization include the flexibility of the procedures and the ability to self-adapt the search for optimum solutions. The algorithm is also parallelizable and can be fragmented into a computer cluster. EC is conceptually simple and easy for non-experts to learn and use.

Evolutionary algorithms are easily transferable from one application to another because only two components are problem dependent: the way that the genotypes are converted to phenotypes and the fitness function [1]. EC techniques are versatile and powerful in solving several analytical problems. They can be applied to solve inverse, nonlinear, and multimodal problems. EC works well when combined with many other AI techniques, such as artificial neural networks and machine learning algorithms. EC algorithms require little or no data to solve problems [15].

Although ECs is generating considerable interest for solving real world problems, they can take a long time to obtain solutions for huge problems because they need to perform several fitness evaluations.

4.7 CONCLUSION

Evolutionary computing is the collective name for a range of problem-solving techniques based on principles of biological evolution. It is considered one of the most promising paradigms of computational intelligence. The field of EC has experienced a tremendous growth in recent years. It is primarily concerned with problem solvers. It has been successfully applied to a wide variety of applications because it can automatically find a feasible solution. It can go above and beyond what is possible with human design. Some have regarded evolutionary computation as the next step in the progress of AI, the creative AI.

More information on evolutionary computing can be found in books in [9,12,16-26] and the following journals that are devoted to it:

- *Evolutionary Computation*
- *IEEE Transactions on Evolutionary Computation*
- *Genetic Programming and Evolvable Machines*
- *Evolutionary Intelligence*
- *Journal of Artificial Evolution and Applications*
- *International Journal of Applied Evolutionary Computation*
- *Swarm and Evolutionary Computation*
- *International Journal of Swarm Intelligence and Evolutionary Computation*

REFERENCES

[1] A. E. Eiben and Jim Smih, "From evolutionary computation to the evolution of things," N at u r e, vol. l 5 2 1, M ay 2 0 1 5, pp. 476-482.

[2] "Evolutionary computation,"*Wikipedia*, the free encyclopedia https://en.wikipedia.org/wiki/Evolutionary_computation

[3] K. L. Fok, T. T. Wong, and M. L. Wong, "Evolutionary computing on consumer graphics hardware," *IEEE Intelligent Systems*, March/April 2007, pp. 69-78.

[4] K. Dutta and S. Sarthak, "Architectural space planning using evolutionary computing approaches: A review," *Artificial Intelligence Review*, vol. 36, 2011, 311–321.

[5] H. Wimmer, "Knowledge guided evolutionary algorithms in financial investing," *Doctoral Dissertation,* University of Maryland Baltimore County, 2013.

[6] M. N. O. Sadiku, Y. Wang, S. Cui, S. M. Musa, "Evolutionary Computing," *International Journal of Advanced Research in Computer Science and Software Engineering*, vol. 9, No. 5, May 2019, pp. 81-83.

[7] A.E. Eiben, "Introduction to Evolutionary Computing II," http://www.cs.vu.nl/~gusz/

[8] V. Oduguwa, A. Tiwari, and R. Roy, "Evolutionary computing in manufacturing industry: An overview of recent applications," *Applied Soft Computing*, vol. 5, 2005, pp. 281-299.

[9] A.E. Eiben and J.E. Smith, *Introduction to Evolutionary Computing*. Berlin: Springer, 2nd ed., 2015.

[10] S. A. Khan et al., "Channel estimation using evolutionary computing techniques," *Proceedings of the IEEE International Conference on Conference: Intelligent Processing Systems,* November 1997.

[11] A.E. Eiben and M. Schoenauer, "Evolutionary computing," *Information Processing Letters,* vol. 82, 2002, pp. 1–6.

[12] A. M. Mora et al. (eds.), *Applications of Evolutionary Computation.* Springer, 2005.

[13] A. I. Marques, V. Garcıa, and J. S. Sanchez, "A literature review on the application of evolutionary computing to credit scoring," *Journal of the Operational Research Society,* vol. 64, 2013, pp. 1384–1399.

[14] G. JayaKrishna and V. Ravi, "Evolutionary computing applied to customer relationship management: A survey," *Engineering Applications of Artificial Intelligence*, vol. 56, 2016, pp. 30–59.

[15] M. Sipper, R.S. Olson, and J. H.Moore, "Evolutionary computation: The next major transition of artificial intelligence?" *Bio Data Mining,* vol. 10, no. 26, 2017.

[16] K. D. Jong, *Evolutionary Computation: A Unified Approach*. MIT Press, 2006.

[17] N. Siddique and H. Adeli, *Computational Intelligence: Synergies of Fuzzy Logic, Neural Networks and Evolutionary Computing.* Chichester, UK: John Wiley & Sons, 2013.

[18] L. Kallel, B. Naudts, and A. Rogers (eds.), *Theoretical Aspects of Evolutionary Computing.* Berlin Heidelberg, Springer-Verlag, 2001.

[19] A. Ghosh and S. Tsutsui (eds.), *Advances in Evolutionary Computing: Theory and Applications.* Berlin Heidelberg, Springer-Verlag, 2003.

[20] M. Preuss, Multimodal Optimization by Means of Evolutionary Algorithms**.** Springer, 2015.

[21] D. Ashlock, *Evolutionary Computation for Modeling and Optimization.* Springer, 2005.

[22] F. Rothlauf et al. (eds.), *Applications of Evolutionary Computing.* Springer, 2005.

[23] A. M. Gujarathi and B. V. Babu, *Evolutionary Computation: Techniques and Applications.* Apple Academic Press, 2016.

[24] M. Tiwari and J. A. Harding, *Evolutionary Computing in Advanced Manufacturing***.** Wiley, 2011.

[25] C. A. C. Coello, D. A. Van Veldhuizen, and G. B. Lamont, *Evolutionary Algorithms for Solving Multi-Objective Problems.* Kluwer Academic Publishers; May 2002.

[26] D. Dumitrescu et al, *Evolutionary Computation.* Boca Raton, FL: CRC Press, 2000.

5

MOLECULAR COMPUTING AND BIOCOMPUTING

It is easier and better to build boys than
to repair men.
- Anonymous

5.1 INTRODUCTION

Conventional computing uses transistors and binary logic for performing operations. However, increasing the number of functional units or speed faces inherent limitations in the number of transistors that can be put in one chip. Thus, progress in silicon technology of integrated networks has come to a standstill in recent years, as fundamental limits are being reached. We therefore seek using molecules as an alternative means of computation. Molecular computers are made of proteins and other molecules rather than silica integrated circuits (ICs). The traditional computing is compared with molecular computing in Figure 5.1 [1]. Although computational devices at the molecular level have been envisioned since the mid 1940s, but it is only recently that actual construction of nano or molecular computers are made for engineering purposes.

Molecular computing (MC) is the science that uses individual molecules to build computer programs. It is encoding, manipulation, and retrieval of information at a molecular level. It is one of the subfields of natural computing and is sometimes referred as DNA computing or biocomputing. It is an interdisciplinary field that uses individual molecules as microscopic switches. It requires the collaboration of polymer chemists, device physicists, electrical engineers, biotech researchers, and futurists [2]. The objective is to produce a von Neumann-type of computer in carbon rather than in silicon because carbon chemistry facilitates the construction of smaller and faster computing devices [3]. Carbon appears to be the element of choice for molecular computing, just as silicon is used for conventional computing.

Molecular computing provides an alternative to computing using silicon ICs. It aims at developing intelligent computers using biological molecules as computational devices. It is a promising means of unconventional computation owing to its capability for massive parallelism. It offers to augment the digital computing with biology-like capabilities. Molecular computing is often made of DNA, RNA, or other bio-molecules. A given computational problem is encoded into DNA like strings which are mixed in a test tube. The computational method has high parallel processing capability [4].

This chapter provides an introduction to molecular computing and biocomputing which are closely related. In this chapter we combine molecular computing and biocomputing as bio-molecular computing. It begins with discussing the basic features of MC. Then it addresses molecular computers, biocomputers, and their applications. It covers their benefits and challenges. The last section concludes with some comments.

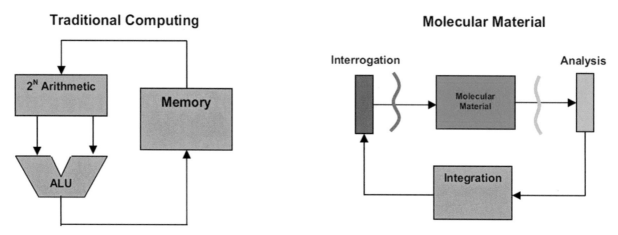

Figure 5.1 Traditional computing compared with molecular computing [1].

5.2 FEATURES OF MOLECULAR COMPUTING

Molecular computers are systems in which molecules or macromolecules individually mediate information processing functions. In other words, molecular computers are information processing systems in which individual molecules play an important role as they are used to build computer programs. (Each molecule operates as a switch.) An important feature of molecular computing (MC) is that it is context-dependent; inputs are processed as physical structures rather bit by bit as in conventional computing. Due to this, molecular computers are suited for processing sensory inputs such as pressure, temperature, and light. Conventional computers handle such tasks poorly [5].

Molecular computing provides several ways of solving difficult mathematical problems. Researchers have recently characterized molecules capable of acting as electronic switches and memory and organic molecules that act as electronic devices. They have initiated a new era of molecular electronics based on organic molecules [6].

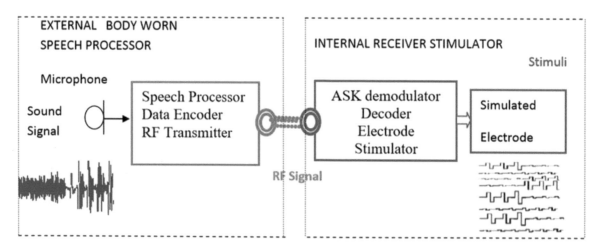

Figure 5.2 Functional block diagram of bio-computing [13].

5.3 MOLECULAR COMPUTERS

Before we can exploit molecular computer, we need to understand how a conventional computer works. Modern computers have three key components: input devices, output devices, and memory. Some of the fundamental features of von Neumann computer are [7]: (1) programming languages exist, (2) universality, (3) sequentially. The key to the next generation of computer technology will lie in our ability to miniaturize the transistor, which is the smallest physical part of a computer processor. The transistor is a switch because it has the ability to change from the "on" and "off" state.

Based on the same principles, but scaled down to the molecular size, molecular devices are currently being developed that can perform switching functions. These devices can be used as a molecular switch to build molecular computers and storage devices [8]. The true potential of molecular electronics could be realized in bringing the world of microelectronics together with the world of biology and molecules. Molecular electronics seeks to build electrical devices to implement computation—logic and memory—using individual molecules. These devices have the potential to reduce device size and fabrication costs, by several orders of magnitude, relative to conventional CMOS.

Molecular computing (also known as biomolecular computing) uses biomolecules.

Several types of molecular switches have been demonstrated. Taking advantage of the small size of molecules within a nanocell, logic devices such as an inverter, a NAND gate, an XOR gate, and a 1-bit adder have been simulated [9]. A team of French scientists has built the first molecular computer using polymers to store data, making each bit 100 times smaller than with current data storage [10]. They will have a lot of challenges scaling-up.

5.4 BIOCOMPUTING

Biocomputing, known also as molecular computing or DNA computing, is a fascinating development at the interface of computer science and molecular biology. It is the application of information technology and computer science to biological problems. It is the process of building computers that use biological materials. It uses systems of biologically derived molecules, such as proteins and DNA, to perform computational calculation [11].

Biocomputing is the use of computers which function like living organisms or contain biological components. Biocomputers use systems of biologically derived molecules such as DNA (or deoxyribonucleic acid) and proteins to perform computation. They are computers made of proteins, genes, and cells; they can perform mathematical operations. Proteins are the fundamental building blocks of life. Cells are made up of proteins. The cell is understood as a computational system; its program resides in DNA. A trillion bio-molecular devices could fit into a single drop of water.

Biological computing can provide a huge parallelism for handling problems in the real world. DNA computers have the capability of high performance computing [12]. The biological computers are mostly used for medical applications. Scientists have been able to create genetic biocircuits that can perform all basic Boolean logic gates: AND, OR, NOT, NAND, NOR, XOR, and XNOR. The functional block diagram of the biocomputing system is shown in Figure 5.2 [13].

We use biocomputer for its multi-processor, cost effective, little waste, high artificial intelligence (AI), self-recovery, and massive memory. DNA Computers can perform massively parallel computation and are highly energy efficient systems [14]. Biocomputing can open up a whole different realm of computing.

Currently, a biocomputer requires hours to return an output. For this reason, biocomputers may never match their digital counterparts in terms of speed. However, significant advances in biology are likely to be made in the coming years and the advances will have impact on biocomputing. The possibility of CPU being replaced by biological molecules remains in the far future.

The challenge for biologists nowadays lies in the de-codification of the complex data they have to handle in order to achieve a better understanding of how our genes shape and how our genome evolved [15]. Scientists that are involved in the biocomputing must take care of legal, moral, and ethical regulations. As engineers and scientists do research on biocomputing, the new discoveries will revolutionize the medical field. Thus, the future for biocomputing is bright. It will lay the foundations for a new era of computing [16].

5.5 APPLICATIONS

Molecular computing or biocomputing has shown great promise in several applications including drug delivery and molecular communication. Bio-molecular computing is a powerful tool for the development of massive parallel computation. A promising area of application of molecular computing is nanotechnology because constructing nanoscale structures requires computation at the molecular level [17]. Due to size limitation, the traditional electromagnetic communication systems cannot be applied for nanonetworks. Molecular computing also has a potential value for building inference engine and expert systems [18].

Quantum-dot cellular automata (QCA) is a revolutionary approach to molecular-scale computing which uses the charge configuration of a set of quantum dots to represent binary information. The basic building-block of QCA devices is the QCA cell. A single molecule can function as a QCA cell. Molecular QCA can be fabricated with a much higher degree of regularity and is on a much smaller size-scale than its metal-dot counterparts. QCA is a paradigm in which general-purpose computing is possible and it holds promise for molecular electronics [19].

Other major applications of molecular computing include control in biological cells, the dynamics of evolutionary processes, the development of new classes of chemical materials, and cognitive computation [20].

5.6 BENEFITS AND CHALLENGES

Molecular materials have a wide range of properties and specific advantages over conventional solid state materials. The main benefit of molecular computing is the potential to pack vastly more circuitry onto a microchip than silicon will ever be capable of. It has the potential for developing massive parallel computing protocol. Molecular electronic systems have the potential of reduced complexity, reduced cost of fabrication, and reduced heat generation. Molecular computers process information encoded in molecules, not in electrical signals. Since molecules are only a few nanometers in size, it is possible to make chips containing billions of components. Molecular devices (with each molecule operates as a switch) are astonishingly easy and potentially cheap to make.

In order for molecular computing to be practical, it must be able to solve problems of a large size. Only few molecular electronic devices can beat silicon devices on both speed and energy efficiency. Lab experiments on molecular computers is expensive, inefficient, and unreliable. Hoping that molecular electronics will catch up with the fast-moving advances of silicon has led to disappointment. In spite of these challenges, the tools used by scientists working in molecular computers are beginning to mature and some of their projects may soon lead to commercial applications. MC has a promising future as our ability to manipulate molecules is improving greatly.

5.7 CONCLUSIONS

Molecular computing as a field is in an early but rapid stage of development. It must be evaluated against the performance of conventional silicon-based computing. Although the field has been gaining a lot of traction, it is currently not possible to build these computers at a large enough scale to substitute silicon. The bold promise of replacing silicon with molecular components is yet to come to reality. Molecular computers are tomorrow's faster and more powerful computers. Molecular self-assembly will be key to engineering nanoscale computers.

More recently, researchers have proposed a hybrid molecular– electronic architecture that plays to the strengths of both domains. Such an ambitious hybrid–electronic design uses a molecular form of near-data processing for massive parallelism [21]. Hybrid automata and molecular robots have been developed. For more information about molecular computing and biocomputing, one is cordially advised to consult [22-29].

REFERENCES

[1]   R. J. Bonneau et al., "A mathematical architecture for molecular computing," *Proceedings of the 36th Applied Imagery Pattern Recognition Workshop*, 3007, pp. 50-86.

[2]   M. N. O. Sadiku, S. M. Musa, and O. M. Musa, "Molecular computing," *Invention Journal of Research Technology in Engineering and Management*, vol. 2, no. 9, September 2018, pp. 68-70.

[3]   M Conrad, "On design principles for a molecular computer," *Communications of the ACM*, vol. 28, no. 5, May 1985, pp. 464-480.

[4]   M. Conrad, "The lure of molecular computing," *IEEE Spectrum*, October 1986, pp.55-60.

[5]   A. F. Rocha, M. P. Rebello, and K. Miura, "Toward a theory of molecular computing," *Journal of Informational Sciences*, vol. 106, 1998, pp. 123-157.

[6]   D. Rotman, "Molecular computing," *Technology Review*, May/June 2000, pp. 53-58.

[7]   M. Conrad, "On design principles for a molecular computer," *Communications of the ACM,* vol. 28, no. 5, pp. 464-480.

[8]   L. Cronin and H. Abbas, "Molecular computers - tomorrow's technology?" January 2007, https://eic.rsc.org/feature/molecular-computers-tomorrows-technology/2020195.article

[9]   J. M. Tour et al., "Nanocell logic gates for molecular computing," *IEEE Transactions on Nanotechnology*, vol. 1, no. 2, June 2002, pp. 100-109.

[10] "World's first molecular computer makes data storage 100 times smaller," https://labiotech.eu/molecular-computer-data-storage/

[11] M. N. O. Sadiku, N. K. Ampah, and S. M. Musa," Biocomputing*," International Journal of Trend in Scientific Research and Development*, vol. 2, no. 6, Sept.-Oct 2018, pp. 1250-1251.

[12] M. Guo, M. Ho, and W. L. Chang, "Fast parallel molecular solution to the dominating-set problem on massively parallel bio-computing," *Parallel Computing*, vol. 30, 2004, pp. 1109-1125.

[13] V. H. Kumar and P. S. Ramaiah, "Configuration of FPGA for computerized speech/sound processing for bio-computing systems," *International Journal of Computer Science Issues*, vol. 8, issue 5, no 3, September 2011, pp. 246-255.

[14] M. S. Ahuja and S. Sharma, "Biological computing: A new paradigm in computing," *Proceedings of the 3rd Conference on Recent Innovations in Science, Technology, Management and Environment*, New Delhi, India, December 2016, pp. 162-166.

[15] D. Herath, C. Lakmali, and R. Ragel, "Accelerating string matching for bio-computing applications on multi-core CPUs," *Proceedings of the IEEE 7th International Conference on Industrial and Information Systems*, September 2012

[16] S. L.Garfinke, "Biological computing," *Technology Review,* May/June 2000, pp. 71-77.

[17] M. Hagiya, "Perspectives on molecular computing," *New Generation Computing*, vol. 17, 1999, pp. 131-151.

[18] P. Wasiewicz et al., "The inference based on molecular computing," *Cybernetics & Systems*, vol. 31, no. 3, 2000, pp. 283-315.

[19] E. P. Blair and C. S. Lent, "Quantum-dot cellular automata: An architecture for molecular computing," *Proceedings of International Conference on Simulation of Semiconductor Processes and Devices*, Sept. 2003.

[20] "Molecular computing," https://doi.org/10.1016/S0065-2458(08)60155-2Get rights and content

[21] D. Carmean, "DNA data storage and hybrid molecular–Electronic computing," *Proceedings of the IEEE*, vol. 107, no. 1, Jan. 2019, pp. 63-72.

[22] T. Sienko et al., *Molecular Computing.* The MIT Press, 2003.

[23] G. Rozenberg, T, Bck, and J. N. Kok, *Handbook of Natural Computing.* Springer, 2011.

[24] W. Chang and A. V. Vasilakos, *Molecular Computing : Towards a Novel Computing Architecture for Complex Problem Solving.* Springer, 2016.

[25] S. K. Shukla and R. Iris Bahar (eds.), *Nano, Quantum and Molecular Computing: Implications to High Level Design and Validation.* Springer India, 2010.

[26] N. Jonoska, G. Paun, and G. Rozenberg, *Aspects of Molecular Computing.* Berlin: Springer-Verlag, 2004.

[27] N. G. Rambidi, *Molecular Computing: Origins and Promises.* Springer, 2014.

[28] P. A. Laplante (ed.), *Biocomputing.* Nova Science Publishers, 2004.

[29] A. J. Ijspeert, M. Murata, and N. Wakamiya (eds.), *Biologically Inspired Approaches to Advanced Information Technology.* Berlin, Germany: Springer, 2004.

6

DNA COMPUTING

People are always blaming circumstances for what they are. I don't believe in circumstances.
The people who get on in this world are
the people who get up and look for the circumstances they want and if they can't
find them, make them.
- George Bernard Shaw

6.1 INTRODUCTION

By definition, computers are machines which receive input, manipulate and store the input, and produce an output. Computers are commonly known to consist of integrated circuits (ICs) mainly constructed of silicon. Development in traditional electronic computers made of silicon will soon reach their limits of speed and miniaturization. DNA computing will solve that problem and serve as an alternative technology.

Chip makers are always looking for ways to produce faster computing speeds. Implementing living systems in computational devices has intrigued researchers for years. Bottom-up manufacturing methods such as molecular self-assembly have no such scale size limits. Molecular computing is computation done at the molecular scale. DNA computing is a class of molecular computing that does computation by the use of DNA molecules. DNA is found in the nucleus of every human cell. DNA computing becomes one of the most appealing alternatives to overcome the silicon computer limitations [1].

Deoxyribonucleic Acid (DNA) and Ribonucleic Acid (RNA) are information carrying molecules. DNA is a complicated molecule with a lot of interesting properties. DNA computing is a special form of computing that employs bio-molecules, mainly DNA, for computational purposes, rather than the traditional silicon-based technologies. A single gram of DNA can hold as much information as a trillion compact disks [2].

DNA computing is also known as molecular computing or bio-molecular computing. It is computing using the processing power of molecular information instead the conventional digital components. It is one of the non-silicon based computing approaches. DNA has been shown to have massive processing capabilities that might allow a DNA-based computer to solve complex problems in a reasonable amount of time.

DNA computing is now an interdisciplinary research field where chemistry, molecular biology, computer science, mathematics, and technology come together.

The aim of this chapter is present DNA computing in simple terms that a beginner can understand. It begins by discussing the historical background for DNA computing. It then explains DNA computers, their operations, and their applications. It addresses their benefits and challenges. The last section concludes with some comments.

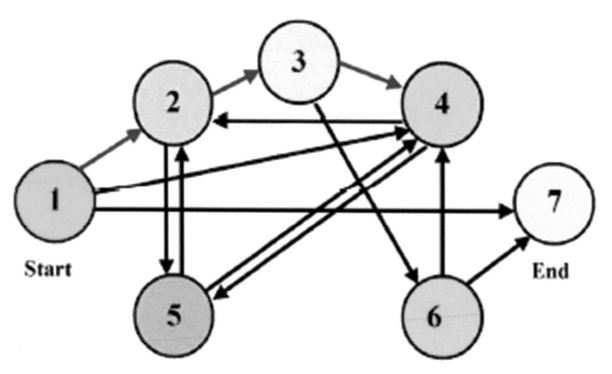

Figure 6.1 The graph in Adleman's experiment [5].

6.2 HISTORICAL BACKGROUND

DNA computing was introduced by Leonard Adleman of the University of Southern California, who demonstrated in 1994 that DNA could be applied in computations [3]. He used DNA to solve a problem that is always cumbersome for traditional computer algorithms, a small instance of the traveling salesman problem, in which the objective is to find the most efficient route through seven cities connected by 14 one-way flights. Adleman solved this problem by creating strands of DNA to represent each flight and then combined them to generate every possible route [4, 5]. The graph in Adleman's experiment is shown in Figure 6.1. Adleman is often called the father of DNA computers.

Adleman's work have set imaginations blazing throughout the world and across disciplines. It introduced a new revolutionary era in the field of computing. In 1997, three years after Adleman's experiment, researchers at the University of Rochester developed DNA–based logic gates, which was seen as a breakthrough. Researchers applied similar ideas to solve difficult problems, like satisfiability problem, the maximal clique problem, the shortest common superstring problem, and even breaking DES.

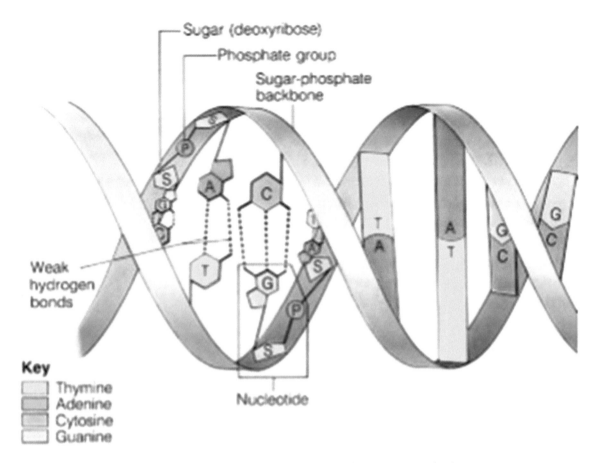

Figure 6.2 Basic structure of a double helix DNA strand [7].

6.3 DNA COMPUTERS

A DNA computer is essentially a nano-computer that uses DNA to store information and perform calculations. In other words, DNA (DeoxyriboNucleic Acid) is the molecule that plays an important role in DNA computing. It is found in every living cell. It is used as a medium to store the genetic information of all living beings. It consists of nucleotides which have four different bases: adenine (A), guanine (G), cytosine (C), and thymine (T). These four bases form the single stranded DNA molecule. The double strand can be separated by heating. Pairs (A, T) and (G, C) are called complimentary. The amount of each nucleotide and the order of their arrangement are unique to every living organism. We define the complement operation as: $\overline{A} = T$, $\overline{T} = A$, $\overline{C} = G$, and $\overline{G} = C$. DNA strands can be regarded as a sequence represented by a combination of four symbols A, G, C, and T. DNA strands are used in encoding the problem, while biological operations are used in simulating the computation [6]. This implies that we have a 4 letter alphabet (A, G, C, T) to encode information, compared with an electronic computer that uses only two digits (1 0) for the same purpose. For example, a single-stranded segment consisting of the base sequence TAGCC will stick to a section of another strand made up of the complementary sequence ATCGG. A strand of DNA bears similarity to a Turing machine's tape. The structure of DNA double helix is shown in Figure 6.2 [7].

The main idea of computing with DNA is to encode data in a DNA strand form and use laboratory techniques known as bio-operations to manipulate DNA strands in a test tube in order to simulate arithmetical and logical operations. DNA is usually double-stranded, consisting of two long strings twisted around each other in a helical form. In a DNA computer, the input and output are both strands of DNA. A DNA computer can solve the problems currently intractable on even the fastest electronic computers.

The DNA computers have the following capabilities/advantages over conventional silicon-based computers [8]:

- *Parallel Computing*: DNA computers by their inherent nature, work on the principle of parallel computing, which allows many calculations to be carried out simultaneously. Each operation on the test tube of DNA is carried out on all strands of the tube in parallel. This massive parallelism of DNA processing is of particular interest in solving complex problems.
- *Computation Ability* : All computers manipulate data by addition and subtraction. A DNA computer should be able to solve a problem with 70 variables and 1,000 AND-OR connections. It over-performs conventional computer in handling "hard" problems due to its inherent massively parallelism nature.
- *Memory*: A DNA computer a memory capacity much larger than any conventional computer. It has a gigantic memory capacity. The information density of DNA is far greater than that of silicon: 1 bit can be stored in approximately one cubic nanometer. A DNA computer can hold about 1×1014 MB of data. Thus, DNA molecules would act like mega-memory.
- *Energy Consumption*: The energy consumption of a DNA computer is reported to be very low when compared to conventional computer. DNA computers can perform 2×10^{19} operations per joule.

Other advantages include light weight and algorithmically fast computing.

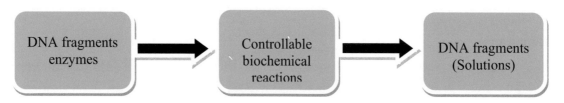

Figure 6.3 DNA computing model [12].

6.4 OPERATIONS ON DNA

A DNA molecule is a long linear polymer. It can exist in either single or double stranded form. Though double stranded DNA appears to be a stable storage medium for information, most proposed DNA computation systems use single stranded DNA for storage and computation. DNA computers perform computations by synthesizing DNA strands and allowing them to react in test tubes. Think of DNA as software, and enzymes as hardware. Putting them together in a test tube allows simple operations when molecules undergo chemical reactions with each [9].

DNA can perform the following primitive biological operations [10, 11]: Anneal, Melt, Ligate, Polymerase Extension, Cut, Destroy, Merge, Separate by Length, and Separate by Subsequence, Append, Mark, Unmark. Some of these are explained below.

1. Synthesis: This is the process of designing and restructuring information in DNA sequence form.

2. Separating: This separates the strands by length using a technique called gel electrophoresis that makes possible the separation of strands by length.

3. Mixing: This combines the contents of two test tubes into a third one to achieve union

4. Ligation. This is a process that joins two DNA molecule ends from the same or different molecules. Ligate is an enzyme that ligates or causes the ends of two DNA strands to stick together.

5. Melting: This breaks apart a double-stranded DNA into its single-stranded complementary components by heating the solution

6. Annealing: This bond together two single-stranded complementary DNA sequences by cooling the solution. This is also called hybridization.

7. Denaturing: A double-stranded DNA molecule is dissolved into single strands by heating the solution to a determined temperature.

8. Amplifying (copying): This makes copies of DNA strands by using the polymerase chain reaction (PCR). PCR is a method for amplifying DNA in vitro.

9. Cutting: This cuts DNA double-strands at specific sites by using restriction enzymes (RE).

10. Detecting: This operation corresponds to an experimental procedure that detects the existence of DNA molecules and confirms presence or absence of DNA.

11. Marking: Two single strands with complementary sequences attach together to make double-stranded DNA. Unmarking is the reverse operation which is done by denaturing which is the separation of double stranded DNA.

12. Destroying: Destroying the marked strands by using exonucleases.

DNA computing model is described in Figure 5.3 [12]. The input consists of DNA fragments and some enzymes. (Enzymes are proteins that accomplish specific functions in the cell.) The output consists of DNA fragments through controllable biochemical reactions [12]. In a DNA computer both the input and output are strands of DNA. DNA computing is a form of parallel computing in that it takes advantage of many different molecules of DNA and tries many different possibilities at once. In order to accomplish DNA computing, it is necessary to have DNA libraries, which are also known as DNA codes. DNA computing can perform reversible DNA computing.

6.5 APPLICATIONS

DNA is a great way to store information. DNA devices have found applications in various ways such as in biosensors for molecular detection, computing, diagnostic applications, in complex nanofabrication, and as potential drug delivery devices.

- *DNA Cryptography:* Cryptography is used widely in information security. Data encryption standard (DES) has been the most widely used cryptosystem. Due to the minuscule size of DNA, DNA cryptography is considered a new field of research which is inspired by DNA computation. DNA cryptography plaintext can be encoded as DNA strands [13].

- *Nanotechnology:* Molecular computers have been a dream of nanotechnology from its inception. Molecular communication aims to enable communication between nano devices in biological environment. DNA nanostructures provide a programmable methodology for bottom-up nanoscale construction of patterned structures. A nanocomputer is a machine that uses DNA to store information and perform complex calculations. Nanotechnology has made it possible to store information in terms of DNA computing-chips.

- *Combinatorial Problems:* DNA computing techniques are suitable to solve the combinatorial problems because they can obtain all the possible solutions. They can realize all the possible combinations of the DNA sequences.

Other areas that can benefit from DNA computing include medicine, data processing, molecular computing, DNA robots, satisfiability problem, graph theory, vertex coloring problem, traveling salesman problem, and finite state problems.

6.6 BENEFITS

DNA computing aims at harnessing individual molecules at the nanoscopic level for computational purposes. DNA itself operates as a fundamental building block for performing computations, building large-scale nanostructures, and constructing individual nanomechanical devices. The major advantages of DNA computation are miniaturization and parallelism over conventional silicon-based machines. It will make computers smaller. The combination of parallelism and miniaturization promises orders more operations per second than current supercomputers. Given its vast parallelism and high-density storage, DNA computing approaches are employed to solve many combinatorial problems [14].

The electronic computers use two digits, 0 and 1, known as binary digits, whereas a DNA strand contains four-letter alphabet that is A, T, G and C which can hold much more information than earlier type of computers. Due to the advancement in nanotechnology, storing information in DNA computing-chips is possible [1].

In recent years, DNA computing has been a research tool for solving complex problems. Originally, the objective of DNA computing, as envisioned by Adleman and others, was to solve numerical problems [15]. The first DNA computers may not likely feature word processing, e-mailing, and programs.

6.7 CHALLENGES

DNA computing has the potential of performing calculations many times faster than most current digital computers. A current limitation is the use of natural enzymes, which act on certain sequences. Right now, the DNA computer can only perform rudimentary operations. Although DNA computer can solve computationally intensive problems, it still takes longer than a desirable time to execute an algorithm. Instead of being "universal", DNA computers are "instance" computers; one can solve a specific problem and in one problem case.

Generating solutions to simple problems may require impractically large amounts of memory. In order to apply DNA computing to a wide range of problems, some procedures for performing primitive operations, such as logic or arithmetic operations, are necessary. Research on DNA computing is still in the proof-of-principle stage. Any practical application is at least some years away. Another drawback of his DNA computer is that it requires human involvement. These limitations must be overcome before DNA computers can replace silicon computers.

6.8 CONCLUSIONS

DNA computing is essentially an area in natural computing based on using biological molecules rather than traditional silicon chips. In DNA computing, computations are performed by biomolecules. DNA computing has emerged in recent years as a catalyst for knowledge transfer between information processing, nanotechnology, and biology. This unconventional computation was proposed as a way of solving a class of computational problems in which the computation time can grow exponentially with problem size [16]. It should not be viewed as competing with the digital computing. It should be regarded as a platform for new applications.

Researchers are still working hard to take advantage of the awesome number-crunching capability of DNA. None of the application is compelling enough to justify the construction of DNA computers. Although DNA computing continues to be an exciting idea, it is still in it's infancy and it is not expedient to attempt to predict the future of a new idea like DNA computing. More information about DNA computing can be found in the books in [17-19].

REFERENCES

[1]   M.N.O. Sadiku, A. E. Shadare, and S.M. Musa, "DNA computing made simple," *Journal of Scientific and Engineering Research*, vol. 3, no. 2, 2016, pp. 116-118.

[2]   S. Tagore et al., "DNA computation: Applications and perspectives," *Journal of Proteomics & Bioinformatics,* vol. 3, 2010, pp. 234-343.

[3]   L. M. Adleman, "Molecular computation of solutions of combinatorial problems," *Science*, vol. 266, 1994, pp. 1021-1023.

[4]   L. M. Adleman, "Computing with DNA," *Science*, vol. 279, August 1998, pp. 54-61.

[5]   A. Regalado, "DNA computing," *Technology Review*, May/June 2000, pp. 80-84.

[6]   G. Steele and V. Stojkovic, "Agent-oriented approach to DNA computing," *Proc. Of Computational Systems Bioinformatics Conference,* 2004, pp. 546-551.

[7]   R. Hasudungan and R. A. Bakar, "DNA computing technique to solve vertex coloring problem," *Proceedings of International Conference on Advanced Computer Science Applications and Technologies,* 2013, pp. 341-345.

[8]   P. Shetty, "DNA computing," *B.Sc. Thesis*, Vishveshwaraiah Technological University, 2009/10.

[9]   K. Hammed, "DNA computation based approach for enhanced computing power," *International Journal of Emerging Sciences*, vol. 1, no. 1, April 2011, pp. 31-37.

[10]   A. Singh and M. Kaur, "DNA computing approach for automated test pattern generation for digital circuits," *International Journal of Systems Science*, vol. 39, no. 2, Feb. 2008, pp. 173-180.

[11]   P. Sugathan, "DNA Computing," *Master's Thesis*, Cochin University of Science and Technology, 2010.

[12]   Y. Huang and L. He, "DNA computing research progress and application," *The 6th International Conference on Computer Science & Education,* 2011, pp. 232-235.

[13]   K. Karimian, "BioCompT: A Tutorial on Bio-Molecular Computing," *Master's Thesis,* University of Cincinnati, 2012.

[14]   Z. Ezziane, "DNA computing: Applications and challenges," *Nanotechnology,* vol. 17, no. 2, 2006, pp. R27-R39.

[15] D.I. Lewin, "DNA computing," *Computing in Science and Engineering*, May/June 2002, pp. 5-8.

[16] Q. Liu et al., "DNA computing on surfaces," *Nature,* vol. 403, Jan. 2000, pp. 175-179.

[17] G. Paun, G. Rozeberg, and A. Salomaa, *DNA Computing: New Computing Paradigms.* Springer, 1998.

[18] Z. Ignatova, I. Martínez-Pérez, and K. H. Zimmermann, *DNA Computing Models.* Springer, 2008.

[19] A. Condon and G. Rozenberg, *DNA Computing.* Springer, 2000.

7

CHEMICAL COMPUTING

A committee is a group of the unwilling, chosen from the unfit, to do the unnecessary.
- Friedrich Engels.

7.1 INTRODUCTION

Information processing based on semiconductor devices is often measured by Moore's law, which states the circuit functionality doubles in less than 2 years time. Since Moore's law cannot be sustained indefinitely, there is a motivation to study alternative, unconventional methods of computing. Unconventional computing is a field of research dedicated to chemistry, physics or biology inspired computational strategies [1].

Computers have transformed the way chemical engineers solve problems. They are valuable tools for engineers. Chemical engineers are being required to solve increasing complex problems, ranging from reactor to pharmaceutical plants. On a bio-molecular level, it is well known that chemical reactions are responsible for processing information in living organisms. Typical examples include signal processing in bacteria, defense coordination, and adaptation in the immune system. A chemical reaction often consists of transformation from one chemical substance (known as reactant) to another substance (called product). During a reaction, molecules are consumed and new ones are formed. The process continues until reaction ceases [2].

In 1989 it was demonstrated that light-sensitive chemical reactions could perform image processing. This led to the emergence of the field of chemical computing. A chemical computer, also called reaction-diffusion computer, is an unconventional computer where data are represented by varying concentrations of chemicals. Chemical computing deals with computing with molecules as well as programming electronic devices using chemical principles.

In the chemical computer version, logic gates are implemented by concentration waves blocking or amplifying each other in different ways [3]. In chemical computing (CC), both the input and output can be optical, electrical or chemical. In CC, emission spectra in chemical reactions are interpreted as logic gates [4].

This chapter briefly introduces chemical computing. It begins with the basic features of chemical computing. Then it discusses some applications of CC, it benefits and challenges. The last section concludes with some comments.

7.2 BASICS OF CHEMICAL COMPUTING

Computing is based on using logic gates, which process a data input to produce an output. Current computers use semiconductors materials for developing logic gates. Until the discovery of Boris Belousov, a Soviet scientist in the 1950s, no one would have thought that chemical reactions could act as logic gates. Chemical computing is computing with molecules as well as to programming electronic devices using principles taken from chemistry. Harnessing the power of chemistry for computing might lead to a new way of coping with the rapidly increasing complexity computational systems.

Chemical computing (CC) ranges from mere simulation of kinetics to the simulation of large reaction systems. Simulation for large-scale problems in chemistry involves the treatment of ordinary differential equation (ODEs) and partial differential equations (PDEs). Popular numerical methods for solving PDEs in chemistry include the method of lines (MOL), Galerkin method, Markov chain Monte Carlo (MCMC) method, finite difference method, and finite element method [5]. The MOL was originally developed by mathematicians and used for solving boundary value problems. It is now widely used in physics, chemistry, and all branches of engineering. The Galerkin method was developed by the Russian engineer B. G. Galerkin in 1915. Markov chains were named after Andrew Markov, a Russian mathematician who invented them. MCMC method is a stochastic approach which involves constructing a Markov chain whose stationary distribution is the same as the equilibrium state of the chemical reaction system. For example, an adaptive MOL package has been used to solve the compressible Navier-Stokes equations including detailed chemistry [6]. COMSOL (formerly known as FEMLAB) is a finite element package which can be used to solve ODEs and PDEs.

7.3 APPLICATIONS

Areas of application of CC include optimum design of chemical reactors, kinetics, thermodynamics, fluid flow, transport, simple mass balances, and ammonia process. For chemical engineers to use CC, they must fully understand the problem to be solved, know the computer programs to use, and verify their solutions with experiment or another technique [7]. Computer programs such as MATLAB, Excel, and COMSOL are readily available. Most of the problems engineers solve today are often intractable and can only be solved with sophisticated software.

7.4 BENEFITS AND CHALLENGES

Chemical computing has enjoyed great success practically and theorertically. The potential benefits of chemical computing are numerous. The main advantage is that with 10^{23} molecules performing computations in parallel, we have a potential for an unheard-of parallelization. Chemical computing is emerging as a promising alternative to simulate the human brain.

Chemical computing faces some challenges [8]:

1. *Efficiency:* How to efficiently obtain chemical programs and their execution;
2. *Scalability:* How do CC paradigms scale up?
3. *Programmability*: Programming a chemical computer;
4. *Robustness*: How to achieve self-adapting and reliable CC systems;

5. *Theory:* How to theoretically describe CC processes.
6. *Speed limit:* CC is limited by the speed of the diffusion of reactions in the medium.

Since computers follow the principle of garbage-in-garbage-out, engineers must find some ways to verify their simulation results. This can be done by comparing the solutions with experiment or those obtained from using a different technique.

Nowadays, engineers need to face the proliferation of hardware and software that can be used to solve their problems. This demands a lot of effort from the users of these tools. They must use these tools wisely.

7.5 CONCLUSION

All living things use chemical reactions to process information on a bio-molecular level, which is robust, adaptive, self-organizing, and evolvable. Numerical solutions of PDEs describing fluid flow, transport, and chemical reaction are at the forefront of chemical computing. Supercomputers have impacted the research and development of chemical sciences. Large-scale simulations are helping chemists understand chemical phenomena [9]. More information on chemical computing can be found in books in [7, 10-12].

REFERENCES

[1] J.Gorecki et al. "Chemical computing with reaction–diffusion processes," *Philosophical Transactions of the Royal Society A*, vol. 373, July 2015.

[2] M. N. O. Sadiku, S.M. Musa, and O. S. Musa, "Chemical computing," *International Journal of Trends in Research and Development,* vol. 5, no. 3, May-June 2018, pp. 162-163.

[3] "Chemical computer," *Wikipedia*, the free encyclopedia https://en.wikipedia.org/wiki/Chemical_computer

[4] R. Stadler, "Molecular, chemical, and organic computing," *Communications of the ACM,* vol. 50, no. 9, September 2007, pp. 43-45.

[5] M. N. O. Sadiku, *Computational Electromagnetics with MATLAB.* Boca Raton, FL: CRC Press, 4th ed., 2019.

[6] P. Deuflhard, U. Nowak, and M. Wulkow, "Recent developments in chemical computing," *Computers & Chemical Engineering*, vol. 14, no. 11, Novermber 1990, pp. 1249-1258.

[7] B. A. Finlayson, *Introduction to Chemical Engineering Computing.* John Wiley & Sons, 2d ed., 2012.

[8] P. Dittrich, "Chemical computing," in J. P. Banatre et al (eds.), *Unconventional Programming Paradigms.* Berlin, Germany: Springer-Verlag, 2005, pp. 19-32.

[9] R. A. Brown, "Supercomputers in chemistry and chemical engineering," http://journals.sagepub.com/doi/pdf/10.1177/109434208800200201

[10] W. Gao, L. Liang, and Y. Chen, *Recent Theoretical Results in Chemical Computing.* LAP LAMBERT Academic Publishing, 2017.

[11] D. C. Young, *Computational Chemistry: A Practical Guide for Applying Techniques to Real-World Problems.* New York: John Wiley & Sons, 2001.

[12] F. Jensen, *Introduction to Computational Chemistry.* Chichester, UK: John Wiley & Sons, 2nd edition, 2007.

8

CELLULAR COMPUTING

If you want others to be happy, practice compassion.
If you want to be happy, practice compassion.
- Dalai Lama

8.1 INTRODUCTION

Over the years, human beings have designed various machines to assist in daily activities. Inspiration from nature can lead us towards new and unconventional methods and tools. The biologically inspired design methods, evolution, and development, have been addressed as possible design methods for cellular computers [1]. Cybernetics assumes that most biological entities can be modelled as machines. A cellular computing system has been proposed as a new system architecture to end the dominance of conventional architectures.

The biological cell, discovered by R. Hooke in 1665, is the smallest sustainable, self-maintaining, and self-reproducing unit of all living organisms. The common feature between a computer and a cell gives rise to a field of study, termed as cellular computing (CC). Cellular computing emerged in 1994 when Adleman demonstrated for the first time how a computation may be performed at a molecular level. Many results have been presented in this field during the past few years by computer scientists, biologists, and complexity theoreticians.

Cellular computing (also known as computation in living cells) promises to provide new means for performing computation more efficiently, in terms of speed, cost, power dissipation, information storage, and solution quality. It is simply a synonym for parallel computing. It may serve as a "backend processor" to a conventional system or as a complete stand-alone loosely coupled system [2].

This chapter provides an introduction to cellular computing. It begins by addressing the features of cellular computing. It highlights some potential applications of CC and the underlying challenges. The last section concludes with some comments.

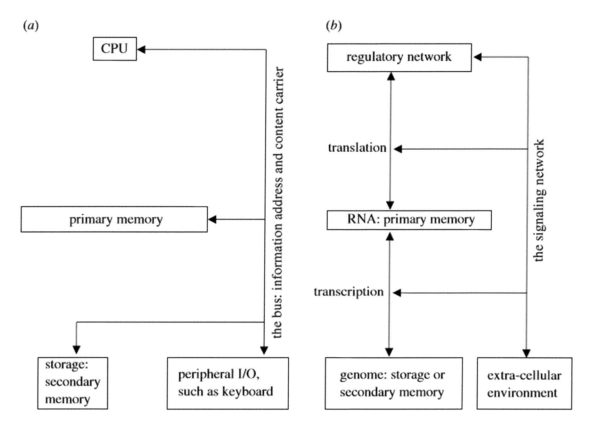

Figure 8.1 A simplistic schematic comparison of the architecture of a computer (a) and a cell (b) [3].

8.2 CONCEPT OF CELLULAR COMPUTING

The biological cell is the smallest independent, self-contained, and self-reproducing unit of any living organism. A cell is so complex that it may be regarded as a multi-layered system or "software system." Cellular computing is a discipline that deals with the analysis and modelling of real cellular processes for the purpose of computation. It essentially uses engineering principles to study and manipulate cells. The similarity between cells and computers provides a useful metaphor from which to obtain powerful predictions about life.

A cellular computer is made of the basic modules which are connected in a regular way. Cells as well as their biological molecules (i.e. proteins, enzymes, etc.) can process information. A simplistic schematic comparison of the architecture of a computer and a cell is shown in Figure 8.1 [3].

A cell is an independently sustainable and self-replicating unit of any organism. At its heart, cellular computing consists of three principles: simplicity, vast parallelism, and locality [4].

- *Simplicity:* The basic computational element in cellular computing is simply the cell. For example, an AND gate is simple. In cellular computing, logic gates are constructed from networks of gene regulation in prokaryotic genomes.
- *Massive Parallelism*: Cellular computing involves parallelism on a much larger scale, with thousands of processors. To distinguish this huge number of processors from that involved in classical parallel computing, the term vast or massive parallelism is used. The intrinsic parallelism of cellular

computer can be used for solving hard problems in a reasonable amount of time. Massive intra-chip parallelism is used to tolerate memory and functional unit latencies.

- *Locality:* Cellular computing is also distinguished by its local connectivity pattern between cells. Locality of interactions implies total absence of global control. A cell can only communicate with a few other cells, most of which are physically close. A local problem involves computing a property that can be expressed in purely local terms, as a function of the local cellular neighborhood.

A typical cellular machine will have the following components [5, 6].

- *Topology:* The study of the interconnection of cells, the topology, is the key to minimal connected fail-soft computers. The tree links consist of a data link say, an address link, a control link, and priority lookahead circuitry to be used for normal operation.
- *Construction:* The cells are made up of a microcomputer CPU and some random access memory (RAM). The microcomputer consists of an arithmetic-logic unit, an instruction register, and a collection of registers. The operation of the microcomputer will be similar to that of the von Neumann computer. It may be programmed in the conventional manner, but has the hardware advantages of the cellular structure.
- *Complexity:* A single cell may be regarded as the simple building block of living organisms. The combination of these simple cells may form a multicellular organism, complex in both its composition and behavior. Multicellular organisms consist of a large number of cells running their own cell cycle in parallel. A major challenge is the creation of an artificial cell. An artificial cell is a minimal cell or in silico 'machine' composed by artificial parts [7].

8.3 APPLICATIONS

Cellular computing has only been investigated from the "top down" perspective. In this computing paradigm, individual cells perform a part of the computation communication taking place only between cells which are within a short distance from one another.

Scientists and engineers have been attempting to construct cell computers because of the diversity of information-processing mechanisms within a cell and the vast parallelism of cellular computing. They have successfully constructed Boolean logic gates (NOT, XOR, AND, NAND gate) and memory elements [8].

The potential applications vary from reprogramming immune cells to fighting infections without inducing harmful side-effects. Cellular automata is the quintessential example of cellular computing. It consists of an array of cells. It is a true parallel interpretation for both development and behavior. It has been used to generate random numbers and perform binary addition. It has also have been applied as a model for studying phenomena in many fields such as physics, biology, chemistry, social phenomena, and computer science. The state-of-the-art now uses multicellular complexes and engineered cell-cell communication. There is the potential applications of introducing logic into cells as lying in fields such as medicine, agriculture, and nanotechnology.

8.4 CHALLENGES

The cellular computing principles are appealing from a hardware point of view. Construction of cellular architectures involves an abstraction from the organisms in nature. The level of abstraction level is dictated by the realistic biological information in the model and the available computation power. A very interesting challenge is the creation of an artificial cell. Since cellular computing is different from the single sequential processor, new programming techniques are needed. Finding local interaction rules to solve global problems poses a challenge for the system designer. The emerging unconventional architectures seem to be creating problems for software implementation. What kind of languages should be chosen and how to map them into a future system are the questions to be answered.

Engineering the first digital control system into a living cell and engineering the system support for experimental cellular engineering into living cells have been challenging. These challenges must be addressed before cellular computing can become a mainstream paradigm.

8.5 CONCLUSION

A cellular system may function as a "backend processor" to a more conventional uniprocessor system or as a complete stand-alone functionally distributed loosely coupled system. Parallel processing appears to be the only way which will improve system performance in the future. Today's reconfigurable technology provides vast parallelism that may be exploited in the design of a cellular computer. More information on cellular computing can be found in books in [9, 10].

REFERENCES

[1]   G. Tufte and P. C. Haddow, "Towards development on a silicon-based cellular computing machine," *Natural Computing,* vol. 4, 2005, pp. 387–416.

[2]   J. Shao and G. E. Quick, "Implementation considerations of mapping lisp onto a cellular computer system*,*" *SIGPLAN Notices*, vol. 20, no. 9, September 1985, pp. 87-93.

[3]   D. Wang and M. Gribskov, "Examining the architecture of cellular computing through a comparative study with a computer," *Journal of Royal Society Interface*, vol. 2, 2005, pp. 187-195.

[4]   M. N. O. Sadiku, N. K. Ampah, and S. M. Musa, "Cellular Computing," *International Journal of Trend in Scientific Research and Development,* vol. 3, no. 6, October 2019.

[5]   G. J. Lipovski, "A varistructured fail-soft cellular computer," *Proceedings of the 1st Annual Symposium on Computer Architecture*, December 1973, pp. 161-165.

[6]   G. Tufte and P. C. Haddow, "Towards development on a silicon-based cellular computing machine," *Natural Computing,* vol. 4, Sprig 2004, pp. 387–416.

[7]   R. Lahoz-Beltra, "Cellular computing: towards an artificial cell," *International Journal Information Theories and Applications,* vol. 19, no. 4, 2012, pp. 313-318.

[8]   J. Smaldon et al., "A computational study of liposome logic: Towards cellular computing from the bottom up," *System and Synthetic Biology*, vol. 4, no. 3, September 2010, pp. 157–179.

[9]   M. Amos (ed.), *Cellular Computing.* Oxford University Press, 2004.

[10] C. Baatar, P. Wolfgang, and T. Roska (eds.), *Cellular Nanoscale Sensory Wave Computing.* Springer, 2014.

9

NANOCOMPUTING

Don't complain. The people who will listen can't do anything about it,
while the people who can do something about it won't listen.
- John M. Hebert

9.1 INTRODUCTION

We have witnessed tremendous speed up in computing power. We are approaching the end of an era in computing: the era where Moore's law reigns, where processing power per dollar doubles every year. To address this problem, two main tracks — evolutionary and revolutionary — are considered [1]:

1. Top-down "More Moore": this track is pushing further the long standing Moore's law-based trend in chip development. It uses conventional lithographic techniques.
2. Bottom-up "Beyond Moore": this features molecular-scale components leading to nanowires, quantum computing, quantum-dot cellular automata based computing, DNA computing, bio-molecular computing, optical computing, etc.

The laws of quantum mechanics and the limitations of fabrication techniques soon will prevent further reduction in the minimum size of today's semiconductor components. As the IC industry starts building commercial devices at such size scales in the 2000s, the term "nanocomputing" has been reserved for device features of only a few nm.

Nanocomputing refers to computing devices built from nanoscale components. It describes computing that uses extremely tiny or nanoscale (one nanometer [nm] is one billionth of a meter) devices. It relates to computing systems which are constructed from nanoscale components. The goal of nanocomputing is to deliver computers smaller than 10 nanometers [2].

This chapter provides a brief introduction to nanocomputing. It begins by taking a closer look at nanotechnology on which nanocomputing is based. It covers the concept of nanocomputing and various nanocomputers. It presents some applications, benefits, and challenges of nanocomputing. The last section concludes with comments.

9.2 NANOTECHNOLOGY

Nanotechnology is the engineering of systems at the molecular or nano scale. It has been called the second Industrial Revolution because of the special properties of materials at the nanoscale. It is a branch of green technology which has the potential to revolutionize many aspects of our lives. It has permeated all sectors of our economy due to the unique properties of materials at the nanoscale. It is transforming the world of materials and its influence will be broad. It will not only initiate the next industrial revolution, it will offer technological solutions. Nanocomputing is part of the emerging field of nanotechnology.

Richard Feynman, a famous Nobel Laureate physicist, is regarded as the father of nanotechnology. Nanotechnology has provided effective processing features, miniaturization from micro to nano obeying the Moore's law, which states that CPU is doubled in performance every 18 months [3]. Nanotechnology is the science of small things—at the atomic level or nanoscale level. It has the idea that the technology of the future will be built on atoms. It has impact on every area of science and technology [4].

Nanotechnology involves imaging, measuring, modeling, and manipulating matter at the nano scale. It covers a wide variety of disciplines like physics, chemistry, biology, biotechnology, information technology, engineering, and their potential applications.

Nanotechnology has a vast range of applications, such as in nanomedicine, nanoelectronics, biomaterials energy production, and consumer products. It is revolutionizing many industry sectors: information technology, homeland security, medicine, transportation, energy, food safety, and environmental science. In medicine, for example, nanotechnologyt is broadening the medical tools, knowledge, and therapies currently available to medical professionals. It can lead to creating smart drugs. Gold nanoparticles are being investigated as potential treatments for cancer and other diseases.

Nanoparticles are used increasingly in catalysis to boost chemical reactions, especially n petroleum refining and automotive catalytic converters. Nanotechnology will likely revolutionize sensor capabilities. Nanosensors and nanoactuators have the potential for improving the capability of sensor networks.

9.3 CONCEPT OF NANOCOMPUTING

Nanotechnology has laid its path in nanocomputing leading towards the solutions for a complex problems. Nanocomputers are electronic computers that contain components with dimensions of only a few nanometers and deal with materials at a molecular level.

They are computing devices of size comparable to a credit card. They may include massive number of devices. They are likely to be up to 10,000 times more densely integrated than today's smallest microcomputers. They can be orders of magnitude faster than current electronic computers. The main objective is to produce computers smaller than 10 nanometers.

With fast-moving nanotechnology, nanocomputers will eventually scale down to the atomic level and will be measured in nanometers. As an alternative to using transistor, nanocomputers might have an entirely new type of circuits or architecture made up of many simple units called cells. Such circuits would consume far less power, increasing battery life and shrinking boxes and fans necessary to cool circuits.

Nanocomputing can be produced by a number of nanoscale structures such as DNA and proteins. Nanocomputers can be built in many ways leading to different kinds of nanocomputers [3,5]:

- *Electronic Nanocomputing:* Nanocomputers can be electronic, where nanolithography is used to create microscopic circuits. These would operate in a manner similar to the way present-day microcomputers work. Nanoelectronics-based intelligent sensors provide a unique opportunity to interface with the physical world at the submicron scale and below. Some see electronic nanocomputers to be most likely future computers.

- *Mechanical Nanocomputing:* This focusses on the microscopic moving parts and works on a purely mechanical basis. Mechanical nanocomputers would use tiny moving components called nanogears to encode information. Nanorobots can operate or be controlled by mechanical nanocomputers. However, mechanical nanocomputer technology has sparked controversy and some consider it unworkable.
- *Chemical/Biochemical Nanocomputing*: A chemical computer is one that processes information by making and breaking chemical bonds. It processes and stores information in the form of chemical structures and their interactions. Both chemical and biochemical nanocomputers would store and process information in terms of chemical structures and interactions.
- *Quantum Nanocomputing*: The quantum nanocomputers rely on quantum physics. They are planned to hold each bit of data as a quantum state of the computer. They combine ideas from classical information theory, computer science, and quantum physics. Instead of storing information in bits as conventional digital computers do, quantum computers use quantum bits or quabits to encode information. Some believe that quantum computers hold the key to true artificial intelligence [6]. Quantum nanocomputer is already under development in the form of single-electron memory (SEM) and quantum dots. The main problem with quantum nanocomputer is instability.

Leading companies such as IBM, Intel, Motorola, and HP are investing heavily in research and development of nanocomputers. Future nanocomputers could be evolutionary, scaled-down versions of today's computers,

9.4 APPLICATIONS OF NANOCOMPUTING

Nanocomputing will allow for the solution of complex real world problems. DNA nanocomputers is suited for application in data processing and can produce faster problem solution through the ability to explore all potential solutions simultaneously. Described below is a sampling of the rapidly growing list of applications of nanocomputing [7]:

- *Medicine:* Nanomedicine, the application of nanotechnology in medicine, draws on the natural scale of biological phenomena to produce precise solutions for disease prevention, diagnosis, and treatment. It is of great concern to store the integrity of the personal medical data especially in the form of images.
- *DNA Nanocomputing*: Nanocomputing can be delivered by various nanoscale structures including biomolecules DNA, and proteins. Practical applications of nanocomputing will require the ability to control and program DNA flexibly. The emerging field of DNA-based nanocomputing methods offers a relief to the problem of utilizing DNA sequences to hide data. DNA based nanocomputing is a growing area of research [8].
- *Quantum Computing:* A nanocomputer is sometimes called a quantum computer. Quantum computing provides computational power at the nanoscale with abilities that reach beyond the limitations of conventional computers. There are many different ways to instantiate quantum computing.

- *Nanorobot or Nanobots*: These will be controlled and managed by nanocomputers. Nano robot can be used for conducting complicated nano surgery on living cells and bacteria. This is possible because of the accurate position control of the nano robot. The nano robot is capable of imaging, manipulating, measuring mechanical properties, and tracking [9].

9.5 BENEFITS AND CHALLENGES

Nanocomputing is an emerging technology that is at the early stage of its development. An exciting anticipation of nanocomputing is the smaller system size it will provide and the ability to construct systems that use many orders of magnitude more components than in the past. Nanocomputing has the unique advantage of being produced to fit into any environment, including the human body. Nanocomputing has proved its usefulness in almost every branch of science and engineering. It has the unique advantage of being created to fit into any environment, including the human body. With nanotechnology, it is possible to tailor the structures of materials at extremely small scales to achieve specific properties. Electronics has greatly benefited from nanotechnology, leading to faster, smaller, and more portable systems that can store large amount of data. Nanomedicine is an application of nanotechnology in medicine that produces precise solutions for disease prevention, diagnosis, and treatment. Nanotechnology offers several means of improving the transportation infrastructure [10]. As nanocomputing evolves, it will be feasible to have more complex and more tightly integrated systems.

Building systems at the atomic scale faces serious challenges. What will nanocomputers "look" like? Upon what operating principles will they function? Do we need drastic new approaches to design hardware and software? How will individual devices be connected together? Once designed, how will these computers be fabricated?

There is a lack of means for large-scale fabrication of nanocomputers. Another challenge is to build a nanoscale memory which can be integrated with existing electronics. A nanoscale network router has the challenge of incorporating high bandwidth I/O at the nanoscale. Embedded controllers are sensitive to power, price, volume, performance, and reliability [5, 11]. When assembling different nano-objects, their locations cannot be controlled. Heat dissipation is another critical challenge facing the realization of nanocomputing technologies. These challenges must be addressed for most nanotechnologies before they can replace conventional CMOS.

9.6 CONCLUSION

Nanocomputers refers to computing systems which are constructed from nanoscale components. Nanocomputing technology has the potential to revolutionize the way that computers are used. Future nanocomputers could be evolutionary, working basically in the same ways as today's computers, but with nanoscale devices. Nanocomputing is still in its infancy.

It is increasingly clear that nanotechnology and nanocomputing will greatly impact the careers of many of our graduate students. Therefore, it is expedient to let graduate students have solid exposure to nanocomputing so that they will be better prepared to solve future problems. More information about nanocomputing can be found in books in [12-19] and many others available in Amazon.com.

REFERENCES

[1]   J. Arlat et al., "Second workshop on dependable and secure nanocomputing," *Proceedings of International Conference on Dependable Systems & Networks,* Anchorage, Alaska, June 24-27 2008, 546-547.

[2]   M. N. O. Sadiku, C. M. Kotteti, and S. M. Musa, "Nano computing: An Introduction," *International Journal of Advances in Scientific Research and Engineering,* vol. 5, no. 3, March 2019, pp. 18-21.

[3]   R. Yadav, C. K. Dixit, and S. K. Trivedi, "Nanotechnology and nano computing," *International Journal for Research in Applied Science & Engineering Technology,* vol. 5, no. X, October 2017.

[4]   M. N.O. Sadiku, M. Tembely, and S.M. Musa, "Nanotechnology: An introduction," *International Journal of Software and Hardware Research in Engineering,* vol. 4, no. 5, May 2016, pp. 40-44.

[5]   M. S. Montemerlo et al., "Technologies and designs for electronic nanocomputers," The MITRE Corporation, 1996. https://www.mitre.org/sites/default/files/pdf/96W0160.pdf

[6]   M. N. O. Sadiku, M. Tembely, and S.M. Musa, "Quantum computing: A primer," *International Journal of Advanced Research in Computer Science and Software Engineering,* vol. 7, no. 11, Nov. 2017, pp. 129-130.

[7]   J. M. Chatterjee and S. Dewangan, "Nanocomputing & its future trends," *International Journal of Advanced Computational Engineering and Networking,* vol. 5, no. 11, Nov. 2017.

[8]   S. Smrithi et al., "Nanocomputing in medicine," *MOJ Biology and Medicine,* vol. 3, no. 1, 2018, pp. 11-12.

[9]   B. Song et al., "Cellular-level surgery using nano robots,*" Journal of Laboratory Automation,* vol. 17. no. 6, 2012, pp. 425–434.

[10] "Benefits and applications," https://www.nano.gov/you/nanotechnology-benefits

[11] "NanoComputing," unknown source.

[12] S. K. Shukla and R. I. Bahar (eds.), *Nano, Quantum and Molecular Computing: Implications to High Level Design and Validation.* Springer, 2004.

[13] N. G. Anderson and S. Bhanja (eds.), *Field-Coupled Nanocomputing: Paradigms, Progress, and Perspectives.* Springer, 2014.

[14] J. B. Waldner, *Nanocomputers and Swarm Intelligence.* Wiley-ISTE, 2013.

[15] J. J. Y. Hsu, *Nanocomputing: Computational Physics for Nanoscience and Nanotechnology.* River Edge, NJ: World Scientific Publishing, 2009.

[16] D. Tyagi and P. Sharma, *Nanocomputing.* Shree Publishers, 2013.

[17] M. M. Eshaghia-Wilner, *Bio-Inspire and Nanoscale Integrated Computing.* Hoboken, NJ: John Wiley & Sons, 2009.

[18] V. Sahni, *Nanocomputing: The Future of Computing.* McGraw Hill Education, 2008.

[19] J. Y. Hsu, *Nanocomputing.* Taylor & Francis, 2017.

10

MEMBRANE COMPUTING

To err is human, but to really foul things up
requires a computer.
– Anonymous

10.1 INTRODUCTION

One may regard the whole history of computer science as a record of continuous attempts to discover, study, and implement computing ideas. Membrane computing (MC) is part of this intellectual journey [1]. It is a young branch of natural computing, which involves computer science, mathematics, biology, and artificial intelligence. It uses cellular membrane systems (seen as computing devices), which are known as P systems after the Romanian scientists Gheorghe Păun who initiated the model in 1998. Since then, the literature of this area has grown very fast.

The basic element of a P system is its membrane structure, which can be a hierarchical arrangement of membranes, as in a cell or a net as in a tissue or a neural net. Life is directly related to cells. The cell is the smallest living thing. Cell means membranes [2]. Biological cell membranes are complex structures that are capable of carrying out diverse functions, functions which are controlled by the membrane's main building blocks (lipids and proteins). The interaction between proteins and lipids is responsible for defining cell membrane function [3].

The chapter provides a brief introduction to membrane computing. It begins by explaining the concept and fundamental principles of membrane computing. It presents membrane systems and some applications of membrane computing. The final section concludes with comments.

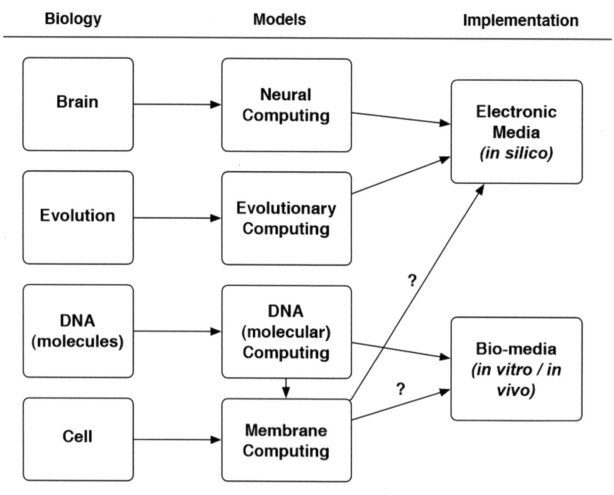

Figure 10.1 The relationship of membrane computing and other branches of natural computing [5].

10.2 CONCEPT OF MEMBRANE COMPUTING

Membrane computing (or cellular computing) is an emerging branch of natural computing, i.e. computing which deals with what is going on in nature and inspired by nature. It is inspired from the functioning of living cells to generate models and simulations of cellular phenomena. It provides distributed parallel computational devices called membrane systems, which are inspired in biological features of living cells.

There has been an ongoing interaction between computer science and biology. Biology has been regarded as a rich source of ideas for creating novel approaches, algorithms, and techniques for solving complex computational problems. Being a model inspired by biology, membrane computing uses objects as transporting mechanisms through membranes. The basic model of MC consists of a hierarchical structure composed by several membranes. All the variants of membrane computing (cell-like, tissue-like and neural-like) share the same simulation structure. Membrane computing is inherently a parallel computing model because communication between the multisets and objects within the regions of a membrane takes place concurrently [4]. The graphic processing unit (GPU) has been used as a parallel tool to implement membrane computing. Another hardware architecture for parallel implementation is the compute unified device architecture (CUDA).

Membrane computing is an unconventional computing model just like quantum computing and DNA computing. It may also be regarded as a branch of molecular computing that aims to develop models and paradigms that are biologically motivated.

Figure 10.1 shows the relationship of membrane computing and other branches of natural computing such as neural computing (based on the processes of the brain), evolutionary computing (based on the processes of evolution), and DNA computing (based on the processes of DNA and called H systems) [5].

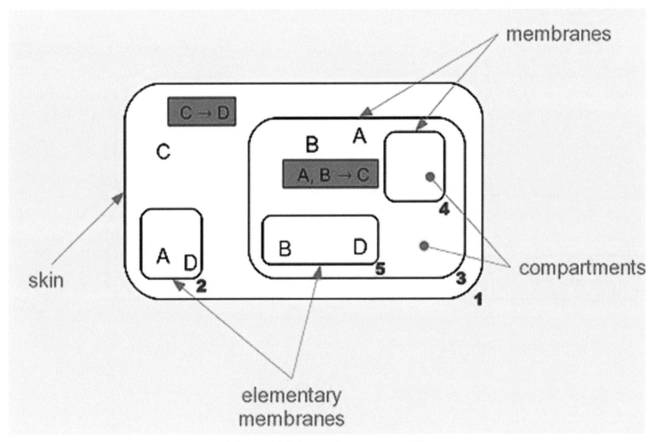

Figure 10.2 A membrane system [2].

10.3 MEMBRANE SYSTEMS

Membrane computing provides class of distributed, parallel, synchronous, and non-deterministic models of computation whose computational devices are called membrane systems. The initial objective of membrane computing was to learn computing ideas (data structures, operations with data, ways to control operations, computing models, etc) from cell biology something useful to computer science. Membrane computing aims to abstract computational model from the structure and functioning of living cells. The computational model is known as membrane system or P system. Generally, there are three components in P system: (i) membrane structure, (ii) multi-sets and (iii) evolution rules [6].

Membrane systems were introduced as a class of distributed parallel computing devices. Membrane computing deals with computing models abstracted from the structure and the functioning of living cells. These models are generally distributed and parallel. Each living cell is being compartmentalized by membranes. A membrane system is shown in Figure 10.2 [2]. Each membrane determines a region; and the region outside the membrane system is called the environment. A membrane without any other membrane inside is said to be elementary. The skin membrane plays only the role of communication environment. The membranes can change their permeability, they can dissolve, and they can divide. They allow certain molecules to pass through (such as waste products to leave) and certain nutrients to enter. Each cell has multisets of objects which follow some evolution rules to decide the next state. The rules dictate how are created, removed, or migrate across regions [7].

10.4 APPLICATIONS

Like other natural computing techniques, MC aims at solving intractable (NP-complete) problems. Over the years, a variety of membrane system (or P systems) have been proposed. Most applications use cell-like P systems and tissue-like P systems.

Membrane computing is employed in global optimization method and is regarded as a optimizing program and strategy. Therefore, it is more like an evolutionary algorithm.

Evolutionary membrane computing explores the interactions between MC and evolutionary computation [8]. Membrane computing can be used to design an optimal infinite impulse response (IIR) filter, which is a challenging optimization problem.

The MC paradigm can also be used to enhance bee algorithm-based feature subset selection method in intrusion detection system. A membrane-inspired feature selection method uses potentials of membrane computing like decentralization, nondeterminism, and maximal parallel computing for feature selection of big cancer data [9].

Other applications of MC are found in computer graphics, linguistics, cryptography, medicine and biology, economics, modeling metapopulation, image segmentation, and approximate optimization [10]. Several software products for implementing P systems on a dedicated hardware have been developed.

10.5 BENEFITS AND CHALLENGES

Membrane computing can be used as a parallel computing device to solve intractable problems. It is useful in medical research, modeling biological processes, and simulating ecosystems. It also finds some applications in areas like economics, computer graphics, and approximate optimization. Membrane systems have been utilized as specification languages for various natural, artificial or engineered systems.

Although membrane computing is useful and has some applications (via usual computers), they do not have yet a bio-lab implementation. Biochemical reactions may deal with inexactitude of the reactives involved in computations since errors may happen when a biochemical reaction takes place. Fuzzy methods have been used to handle this kind of inexactitude [11].

10.6 CONCLUSION

Recent advances in molecular and theoretical biology as well as in mathematical and computational sciences will provide accurate, systemic, and alternative models of complex biological phenomena in the near future. Membrane computing is a bio-inspired computing model, whose devices are called membrane systems or P systems. Membrane computing is a new unconventional, fascinating computing model that abstracts from the structure and functionality of biological entities like living cells and tissues.

It studies the properties and applications of theoretical computing devices known as P systems, which are basically an abstraction of the functioning of a living cell.

Membrane systems have been used in recent years as modelling vehicles for various biological systems. Evolutionary membrane computing is a new research direction of membrane computing that aims to explore the complex interactions between membrane computing and evolutionary computation [8]. More information about membrane computing can be found in books in [12-31] and the journal exclusively devoted to it: *Journal of Membrane Computing*.

REFERENCES

[1] G. Paun and M. J. Pérez-Jiménez, "Membrane computing: Brief introduction, recent results and applications," *BioSystems*, vol. 85, 2006, pp. 11-22.

[2] G. Paun, "Membrane computing," http://www.scholarpedia.org/article/Membrane_Computing

[3] R. Askhar, "Unlocking the secrets of cell membranes," *ACM SIGCAS Computers & Society,* vol. 46, no. 2, August 2016, pp. 5-8.

[4] K. I. Rufai, R. C. Muniyandi, and Z. A. Othman, "Improving bee algorithm based feature selection in intrusion detection system using membrane computing," *Journal of Networks*, vol. 9, no. 3, March 2014, pp. 523-529.

[5] S. Woodworth, 'Computability limits in membrane computing," *Doctoral Dissertation,* University of California, Santa Barbara, September 2007.

[6] Z. Gao and C. Zhang, "MCIR: A multi-modal image registration algorithm based on membrane computing," *Proceedings of International Conference on Computing Intelligence and Information System,* 2017, pp. 263-269.

[7] M. N. O. Sadiku, A. E. Shadare, and S. M. Musa, "Membrane computing: A gentle introduction," *International Journal of Advances in Scientific Research and Engineering,* vol. 5, no. 6, June 2019, pp. 13-15.

[8] G. Zhang et al., "Evolutionary membrane computing: A comprehensive survey and new results," *Information Sciences,* vol. 279, 2014, pp. 528–551.

[9] N. Elkhani and R. C. Muniyandi, "Membrane computing to model feature selection of microarray cancer data," *Proceedings of the ASE Big Data & Social Informatics*, Kaohsiung, Taiwan, October 2015.

[10] G. Paun, "A quick introduction to membrane computing," *The Journal of Logic and Algebraic Programming*, vol. 79, 2010, pp. 291–294.

[11] J. Casasnovas et al., "An approach to membrane computing under inexactitude," http://psystems. disco.unimib.it/download/fuzzymem.pdf

[12] G. Paun, *Membrane Computing: An Introduction.* Berlin: Springer, 2002. (Also available in Chinese.)

[13] P. Frisco, M. Gheorghe, and M. J. Pérez-Jiménez, *Applications of Membrane Computing in Systems and Synthetic Biology.* Springer, 2014.

[14] G. Paun, G. Rozenberg, and A. Salomaa, *The Oxford Handbook of Membrane Computing.* New York: Oxford University Press, 2010.

[15] G. Rozenberg et al. (eds.), *Membrane Computing.* Springer, 2015.

[16] A. Ionescu, *Membrane Computing: Traces, Neural Inspired Models, Controls.* OmniScriptum, 2009.

[17] G. Zhang, M. J. Pérez-Jiménez, and M. Gheorghe, *Real-life Applications with Membrane Computing.* Springer, 2017.

[18] P. Chinedu *A Study of the Application of Multiset to Membrane Computing.* LAP Lambert Academic Publishing, 2011.

[19] C. C. Calude and G. Paun, *Computing with Cells and Atoms; An introduction to quantum, DNA, and Membrane Computing.* Taylor & Francis, 2001.

[20] A. G. Florea and C. Buiu, *Membrane Computing for Distributed Control of Robotic Swarms: Emerging Research and Opportunities.* IGI Global, 2017.

[21] G. Ciobanu, M. J. Pérez-Jiménez, and G. Păun (eds.), *Applications of Membrane Computing.* Springer, 2006.

11

SOFT COMPUTING

Man is still the most extraordinary computer of all.
–John F. Kennedy

11.1 INTRODUCTION

Soft computing (SC) is a newly emerging multidisciplinary field. It is a collection of computational techniques, such as expert systems, fuzzy logic, neural networks, and evolutionary algorithms, which provide information processing capabilities to solve complex practical problems. The major benefit of SC lies in its ability to tolerate imprecision, uncertainty, partial truth, and approximation in processing imprecise and inaccurate information and simulating human decision making at low cost [1, 2].

The principal premise of soft computing (SC) is that we live in a world that is imprecise and uncertain. Soft computing refers to the use of "inexact" or approximate solutions to computationally hard tasks. The role model for soft computing is the human mind. As shown in Figure 11.1 [3], SC is different from traditional (hard) computing in that it is tolerant of imprecision, uncertainty, and approximation. It deals partial truth to generate practical, low-cost (in space and time complexity), low-precision (approximate), good solutions [4].

The term "soft computing" was coined in 1991 by Professor Lofti A. Zadeh of the University of California, Berkeley. Since then, the area has experienced rapid development. Soft Computing became a discipline within Computer Science in the early 1990s. The terms "machine intelligence" and "computational intelligence" have been used to have close meaning as soft computing.

As shown in Figure 11.2 [5], soft computing is a consortium of techniques including artificial neural networks (ANNs), evolutionary computation (EC), genetic algorithms (GAs), machine learning (ML), fuzzy logic (FL), cellular automata (CA), chaos theory (CT), swarm intelligence (SI), probabilistic reasoning (PR), support vector machines (SVMs), and their hybrids [6]. The common denominator of these methods is their departure from classical approaches based on Boolean logic, analytic models, and deterministic search. Since each technique has its own limitations, integration of the techniques helps one to utilize the advantages of each [7]. SC produces an approximate and low-cost solution to hard problems.

This chapter provides a gentle introduction on soft computing. It starts with providing the basic features of soft computing. Then it covers some soft computing techniques. It presents some applications, benefits, and challenges of SC. The last section concludes with some comments.

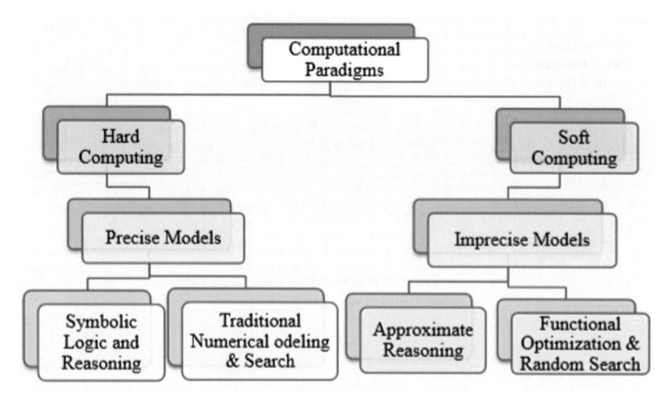

Figure 11.1 Hard and soft computing [3].

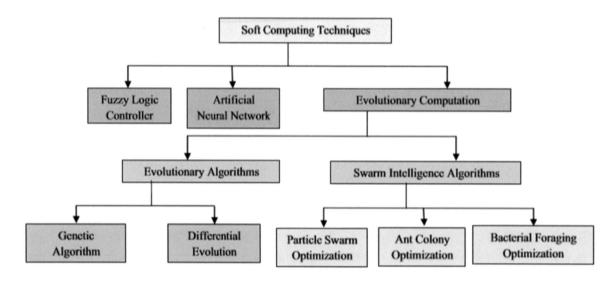

Figure 11.2 Principal constituents of soft computing [5].

11.2 BASIC FEATURES OF SC

Hard (traditional) computing emphasizes precision, certainty, and rigor, while soft computing requires that computation, reasoning, and decision making exploit the tolerance for imprecision and uncertainty wherever possible. It is a conventional computing approach which requires precisely stated analytical model and takes very large computation time. Hard computing methods are typically easier to apply. Also the stability of resulting solutions is highly predictable and the computational burden of practical algorithms is typically low Today, we have microwave ovens, washing machines, cameras, and many other products that manifest an impressive capability to reason, make intelligent decisions, adapt to changes in the operating conditions, and learn from experience [8].

Soft computing may be regarded as a collection of techniques and methods for handling real life situations in the same way as humans deal with them, i.e. using intelligence, common sense, analogies, etc. SC is therefore a family of methods based on approximate reasoning. The major characteristics of SC include [9]:

- Ill-structure object, whose mathematic model is hard to build
- Approximation, imprecision, uncertainty, and partial truth
- Insensitivity to initial values of parameters or initial information
- Parallel-structured-based algorithm
- Result is not optimum, but satisfying

The main aim of soft computing is that computation, reasoning and decision-making should exploit the tolerance for approximation, imprecision, uncertainty, and partial truth to obtain low-cost, low-precision solutions [10]. SC provides the means to build intelligent machines, solve nonlinear problems, and represent ambiguity in human behavior with uncertainty in real life. An increasing number of problems in multimedia, machine learning, and computer vision are naturally fault tolerant. Such problems provide approximate results that have subjective interpretations [11].

11.3 SOFT COMPUTING TECHNIQUES

Soft computing techniques (i.e. tools) provide an ability to make decisions and learning from the reliable data or expert's experience. The principal components of soft computing include artificial intelligence (AI), artificial neural network (ANN), fuzzy logic (FL), evolutionary algorithms (EA), genetic algorithm (GA), machine learning (ML), and probabilistic reasoning (PR), particle swarm optimization (PSO), and hybrid systems. Soft computing techniques generally resemble biological processes more closely than traditional techniques. They are briefly explained as follows [12].

- *Artificial Intelligence:* AI is a broad topic, consisting of different fields, from machine vision to expert systems. AI will set the trend in the future of computing. Machines equipped with AI can be made to thoughtfully plan towards the fulfilment of tasks. They can be made to act quickly, unaffected by emotion. The major concern regarding the application of AI is about ethics and moral values.
- *Artificial Neural Network.* This is information processing inspired by the biological brain. The ANN is essentially composed of three layer: input, hidden and output layers where each layer can have number of nodes. The ANN is trained using the neuron by neuron learning algorithm. The learning process is either supervised and unsupervised. The most popular learning algorithm is the error-back propagation algorithm. Neural networks are very powerful as nonlinear signal processors. A typical artificial neural network is shown in Figure 11.3 [13].
- *Fuzzy Logic:* This is a mathematical logic, which attempts to solve problems with an imprecise spectrum of data. Fuzzy logic imitates what happens in the real world, where information is often ambiguous or imprecise. An organized way of dealing with imprecise data is called fuzzy logic. Fuzzy logic is based on the "degree of truth" for representing human knowledge that is may vary

from 0 to 1. It is relatively easy to design but number of inputs in the system are significantly limited. Soft computing and fuzzy logic mimic the ability of the human mind to use modes of reasoning that are only approximate rather than exact.

- *Evolutionary Computation*: This is an area of research within computer science, which draws inspiration from the process of natural evolution. Evolutionary computation offers practical advantages to the researchers facing difficult optimization problems. Thus evolutionary computing is needed for developing automated problem solvers, where the most powerful natural problem solvers are human brain and evolutionary process (that created the human brain). The algorithms involved in evolutionary computing are termed as evolutionary algorithms (EA). The applications of evolutionary computing include bio informatics, combinatorial optimization, data mining, and machine learning.

- *Genetic Algorithm*: This is a subset of evolutionary computation. It takes all its inspiration from nature. The concept idea of genetic algorithm is to mimic the natural selection in nature where the fittest elements are chosen.

- *Support Vector Machines:* These are a set of related supervised learning methods used for classification and regression. An SVM training algorithm builds a model that predicts whether a new example falls into one category or the other [14].

- *Probabilistic Reasoning*: Probabilistic reasoning is often used in dealing with uncertain and incomplete data in artificial intelligence. The aim of probabilistic reasoning is to combine the capability of probability theory with the capability of deductive logic to exploit structure [15].

Today, these computing techniques are used in classification, regression, pattern recognition, medicine, system modeling, decision making, pattern, and food engineering. These will be expatiated in the next section.

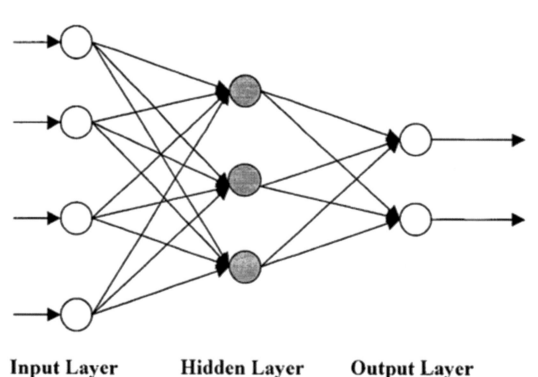

Input Layer   Hidden Layer   Output Layer

Figure 11.3 A typical artificial neural network with one hidden layer [13].

11.4 APPLICATIONS

Soft Computing represents a significant paradigm shift in the aims of computing. It is causing a major breakthrough in science and engineering because it can solve problems that are intractable by conventional analytic methods. SC approaches are capable of adapting themselves to problem domain. There are many potential applications of soft computing methodologies, which includes pattern recognition, adaptive control system, robotics, data mining, bioinformatics, information security, drug design, effort estimation, precipitation estimation and forecasting, video processing, aerospace, pattern recognition by clustering, document clustering, customer segmentation, supply chain management, postal address mapping, clinical neurology, healthcare, agricultural and biological engineering, disease classification, welding process, traffic control systems, several prediction problems, medical diagnosis, computer vision, machine intelligence, weather forecasting, and network optimization. We will discuss some of these in detail.

- *Intelligent machines*: An intelligent machine depends on computational intelligence. Its primary components include sensors, actuators, controllers, and the communication backbone. Soft computing is an important branch of computational intelligence, where soft computing techniques are used to mimic the reasoning and decision making of a human being [16].

- *Process Control*: Process control is important in any industry. Conventional control systems suffer from transient and steady state problems like overshoot, settling time and rise time. Soft computing has become a major research and study area in automatic control engineering. It either replaces a human to perform a control task or it borrows ideas from how biological systems solve problems and applies it to control processes. SC has provided a means for the development of industrial process controllers. Two soft computing techniques (fuzzy logic and genetic algorithms) are used for process controller. Fuzzy logic is a universal approximator that can be used for modelling highly non-linear, unknown controllers or processes. Genetic algorithms can be applied to the process controllers for their optimization using natural operators [17].

- *Robotics*: This is an emerging field which is based on human thinking and behavior. Autonomous robots are a typical example of systems affected by uncertainty. Robotics is a domain in which knowledge about the environment is inherently weak and incomplete. The features of fuzzy control, neural networks and evolutionary algorithms are of particular benefit to the type of problems emerging in behavior based robotics [18].

- *Home Appliances:* Soft computing has been used in consumer appliances since the late 1980s. A fuzzy logic-based controller for controlling the refrigerant distribution in a home air conditioner has been proposed. Soft computing techniques have also been applied successfully in food preparing appliances, such as rice cookers and microwave ovens. The main objective of such designs is to produce tasty food. Soft computing control is used to mimic the characteristics of traditional rice cookers and experienced cooks [19].

- *Business*: Soft computing techniques can be used in an uncertain business decision environment to deal with the vagueness of human thought. There are many applications of soft computing in business and economics including marketing, finance, electronic business, stock marketing forecasting, and foreign exchange rate prediction. In the arena of investment trading, the traditional computing typically gives way to soft computing, as the rigid conditions applied by traditional computing cannot be met [20].

- *Healthcare*: Soft computing approaches have been applied in healthcare for effectively diagnosing the diseases and obtaining better results in comparison to traditional approaches. The use of SC in healthcare provides better aids that assist the physician in many cases, rapid identification of diseases, and diagnosis in real time [21]. Various methods of building cancer predictors have been proposed such as support vector machines and artificial neural networks.

SC methods are also being used in several domestic, commercial and industrial applications.

11.5 BENEFITS AND CHALLENGES

Unlike hard (conventional) computing which strives for exactness, soft computing has the benefit of being tolerant of imprecision, uncertainty, partial truth, and approximation. Soft computing has found wide applications. due to it strong learning and good tolerance of uncertainty and imprecision. It enables the solution of nonlinear problems, whose mathematical models are not available. Soft computing methods are preferred over conventional control system design, for problems that are difficult to describe by analytical models. Such problems often originate in the human mind with emotions and subjectivity. For example, how to determine an appropriate temperature of a room that will make everyone feel comfortable. The robustness, cost effectiveness, adaptability, and simplicity are the few characteristics of the soft computing. It introduces cognition, recognition, understand, learning, and other human skills into computing [22].

Training ANNs is often difficult and time consuming. Although ANNs have been around for over three decades, we still have difficulties training them. Popular training algorithms are not capable of tuning neural networks to proper accuracy without losing generalization abilities. In industrial practice, one can be frustrated using ANN due to wrong learning algorithms and wrong neural network. Determination of fuzzy rules for many problems has not been quite feasible by an expert human. As a way of overcoming these challenges, fusing soft computing and hard computing algorithms has been proposed [23].

11.6 CONCLUSION

Soft computing is an evolving combination of techniques which exploits tolerance for imprecision, uncertainty, and partial truth to generate robust, tractable, and low-cost solutions. It is becoming popular due to its ability to handle complex, dynamic, and non-linear real-world problems involving imprecision, vagueness, and high dimensionality. Consequently, interest in SC has simulated the development of new methods in neural networks, fuzzy logic, genetic algorithms, and other related areas. The impact of soft computing will be felt increasingly among scientists in coming years since it represents a significant paradigm shift in the aims of computing.

With the need to build intelligent systems, the recognition of the Internet of things (IoT), and the advent of high performance digital processors, the application of SC techniques is likely to grow considerably in the future. It will definitely play a crucial role in the future development of science and technology. In view of this, students should be exposed to soft computing [24].

More information on soft computing is available in [[12, 22, 25-45]] and other books at Amazon.com. One should also consult the following journals exclusively devoted to SC:

- *Soft Computing*
- *Applied Soft Computing*
- *Journal of Soft Computing and Applications*
- *International Journal of Artificial Intelligence and Soft Computing*
- *Applied Computational Intelligence and Soft Computing*
- *Journal of Soft Computing and Decision Support Systems*
- *International Journal of Soft Computing*
- *International Journal of Soft Computing and Networking*
- *International Journal of Soft Computing and Engineering*
- *Aloy Journal of Soft Computing and Applications,*
- *ICTACT Journal on Soft Computing,*
- *Intelligent Automation & Soft Computing,*
- *International Journal of Advances in soft computing and its application*
- *The International Journal of Soft Computing and Software Engineering*
- *Journal of Multiple-Valued Logic and Soft Computing*

REFERENCES

[1] M. N. O. Sadiku, Y. Wang, S. Cui, S. M. Musa, "Soft computing: An introduction," *International Journal of Advanced Research in Computer Science and Software Engineering,* vol. 8, no. 6, June 2018, pp. 63-65.

[2] D. Ibrahim, "An overview of soft computing," *Procedia Computer Science*, vol. 102, 2016, pp. 34-38.

[3] "Chapter 1: Introduction," Unknown Source.

[4] "Soft computing," *Wikipedia,* the free encyclopedia https://en.wikipedia.org/wiki/Soft_computing

[5] M. Balamurugan, S. K. Sahooa, and S. Sukcha, "Application of soft computing methods for grid connected PV system: A technological and status review," *Renewable and Sustainable Energy Reviews*, vol. 17, 2017, pp. 1493-1508.

[6] M. Ko, A. Tiwari, and J. Mehnen, "A review of soft computing applications in supply chain management," *Applied Soft Computing*, vol. 10, 2010, pp. 661-674.

[7] S. Mitra, R. Das, and Y. Hayashi, "Genetic networks and soft computing," *IEEE/ACM Transactions on Computational Biology and Bioinformatics*, vol. 8, no. 1, January/February 2011, pp. 94-107.

[8] L. A. Zadeh, "Fuzzy logic, neural networks, and soft computing," *Communications of the ACM,* vol. 37, no. 3, March 1994, pp. 77-84.

[9] X. Li, D. Ruan, and A. J. van der Wal, "Discussion on soft computing at FLINS'96," *International Journal of Intelligent Systems*, vol. 13, 1998, pp. 287-300.

[10] S. Mitra and Y. Hayashi, "Bioinformatics with soft computing," *IEEE Transactions on Systems, Man, and Cybernetics--Part C: Applications and Reviews*, vol. 36, no. 5, September 2006, pp. 616-635.

[11] D. S. Khudia and S. Mahlke, "Harnessing soft computations for low-budget fault tolerance," *Proceedings of the 47th Annual IEEE/ACM International Symposium on Microarchitecture,* 2014, pp. 319-330.

[12] M. Panda, *Soft Computing: Concepts and Techniques.* New Delhi, India: Universal Science Press, 2014.

[13] H, H. Dang, "A soft computing approach to the autonomous space rendezvous problem," *Doctoral Dissertation,* New Mexico State University, December 2008.

[14] A. B. Kurhe et al., "Soft computing and its applications," *BIOINFO Soft Computing,* vol. 1, no. 1, 2011, pp-05-07.

[15] U. Kumari, "Soft computing applications: A perspective view," *Proceedings of the 2nd International Conference on Communication and Electronics Systems,* 2017, pp. 787-789.

[16] C. W. de Silva, "The role of soft computing in intelligent machines," *Philosophical Transactions A: Mathematical, Physical and Engineering Sciences, vol. 361, August 2003,* pp. 1748-1780.

[17] R. Malhotra, N. Singh, and Y. Singh, "Soft computing techniques for process control applications," *International Journal on Soft Computing,* vol.2, no.3, August 2011, pp. 32-44.

[18] F. Hoffmann, "An overview on soft computing in behavior based robotics," *International Fuzzy Systems Association World Congress,* 2003, pp 544-551.

[19] Y. Dote and S. J. Ovaska, "Industrial applications of soft computing: A review," *Proceedings of the IEEE,* vol. 89, no. 9, Sept. 2001, pp. 1243 – 1265.

[20] R. A. Dhopte, Z. Ali, and H. S. Dhopte, "Recent trends and applications of soft computing: A survey," *International Journal of Computer Science and Applications,* vol. 6, no.2, April 2013, pp. 243-247.

[21] S. Gambhir, S. K. Malik, and Y. Kumar, "Role of soft computing approaches in healthcare domain: A mini review," *Journal of Medical Systems,* vol. 40, 2016.

[22] D. Simic, S. Simic, and I. Tanackov, "An approach of soft computing applications in clinical neurology," in E. Corchado, M. Kurzynki, and M. Wozniak (eds.), *Hybrid Artificial Intelligent Systems.* Berlin: Springer-Verlag, 2011, pp. 429-436.

[23] S. J. Ovaska, A. Kamiya, and Y. Chen, "Fusion of soft computing and hard computing: Computational structures and characteristic features," *IEEE Transactions on Systems, Man, and Cybernetics—Part C: Applications and Reviews,* vol. 36, no. 3, May 2006, pp. 439-448.

[24] L. Magdalena, "Soft computing for students and for society," *IEEE Computational Intelligence Magazine,* February 2009, pp. 47-50.

[25] S.K. Pal et al. (eds.), *Handbook on Soft Computing for Video Surveillance.* Boca Raton, FL: CRC Press, 2012.

[26] A. D. Nola (ed.), *Soft Computing: A Fusion of Foundations, Methodologies and Applications.* Berlin: Springer-Verlag, 2018.

[27] K. S. Ray, *Soft Computing and Its Applications: Volumes One and Two.* Apple Academic Press, 2014.

[28] N. Dey et al. (eds.), *Soft Computing Based Medical Image Analysis.* Elsevier, 2018.

[29] N. K. Sinha and M. M. Gupta (eds.), *Soft Computing and Intelligent Systems.* Elsevier, 2000.

[30] A. Majumdar (ed.). *Soft Computing in Textile Engineering.* Woodhead Publishing, 2011.

[31] A. K. Nagar (ed.), *Handbook of Research on Soft Computing and Nature-Inspired Algorithms.* Information Science Reference, 2017.

[32] S. J. John (ed.), *Handbook of Research on Generalized and Hybrid Set Structures and Applications for Soft Computing.* Information Science Reference, 2016.

[33] D. K. Pratihar, *Soft Computing.* Alpha Science International, 2007.

[34] S. Mitra and T. Acharya, *Mining: Multimedia, Soft Computing, and Bioinformatics*. Hoboken, NJ: John Wiley & Sons, 2003.

[35] E. Snachez, T. Shibata, and L. A. Zadeh (eds.*), Genetic Algorithms and Fuzzy Logic Systems: Soft Computing Perspectives*. Singapore: World Scientific Publishing, 1997.

[36] D. K. Chaturvedi, *Soft Computing: Techniques and Its Applications in Electrical Engineering*. Springer, 2008.

[37] R. A. Aliev, B. Fazlollahi, and R. R. Aliev, *Soft Computing and Its Applications in Business and Economics*. Springer, 2004.

[38] A. Tettamanzi and M. Tomassini, *Soft Computing: Integrating Evolutionary, Neural, and Fuzzy Systems*. Springer, 2001.

[39] S. K. Pal, T. D. Dillon, and D. S. Yeung (eds.), *Soft Computing in Case Based Reasoning*. Springer, 2001.

[40] S. K. Pal, A. Ghosh, and M. K. Kundu (eds.), *Soft Computing for Image Processing*. Springer, 2000.

[41] F. Crestani and G. Pasi (eds.), *Soft Computing in Information Retrieval: Techniques and Applications*. Springer, 2000.

[42] M. Thuillard, *Wavelets in Soft Computing*. Singapore: World Scientific Publishing, 2001.

[43] J. S. R. Jang, C. T. Sun, and E. Mizutani, *Neuro-Fuzzy and Soft Computing—A Computational Approach to Learning and Machine Intelligence*. Englewood Cliffs, NJ: Prentice-Hall, 1997.

[44] N. R Pal (ed.), *Pattern Recognition in Soft Computing Paradigm*. Singapore: World Scientific Publishing, 2001.

[45] R. Ali and, M. M. S. Beg (eds.), *Applications of Soft Computing for the Web*. Springer, 2017.

12

AUTONOMIC COMPUTING

Computations: No one believes them,
except the person who makes them.
Experiments: Everyone believes them, except the person who made them.
- B. Munk

12.1 INTRODUCTION

The complexity of conventional systems within the enterprise is growing at an exponential rate. This is the number-one headache of industry leaders. Computing systems are increasingly becoming too complex for humans to manage effectively. As a result, systems grow and change, people make mistakes, and programs crash. The solution to this problem or crisis is a technology that manages itself. Autonomic computing fits in here as computing operations that can run without the need for human intervention.

Autonomic computing is the discipline that seeks to learn from biological systems such as our bodies. An autonomic system minics the human body's autonomic nervous system. It is a self-managing system without human intervention by users. It constantly checks and optimizes its status and automatically adapts itself to changing conditions.

As shown in Figure 12.1, computing systems have reached a level of complexity where it is difficult for human operators to keep them operational [1]. There are two categories of computing systems [2]: (1) Imperative computing system which is a conventional passive system that implements deterministic controlled behaviors, (2) Autonomic computing system which is an emerging intelligent system that autonomously carries out robotic and interactive actions. Autonomic systems can control and manage themselves automatically with minimal intervention by users. In an autonomic system, the human operator does not control the system directly, but defines general rules that guide the self-managing system.

Autonomic computing (AC) is a new paradigm for designing, developing, deploying, and managing complex systems such as clouds by imitating the strategies used by biological systems [3]. Research on autonomic computing includes several disciplines such as computer science, psychology, economics, artificial intelligence, and biology.

This chapter provides a brief introduction on autonomic computing. It begins by discussing the fundamentals and properties of AC systems. It then discusses some of the applications, benefits, and challenges of autonomic systems. The last section concludes with some comments.

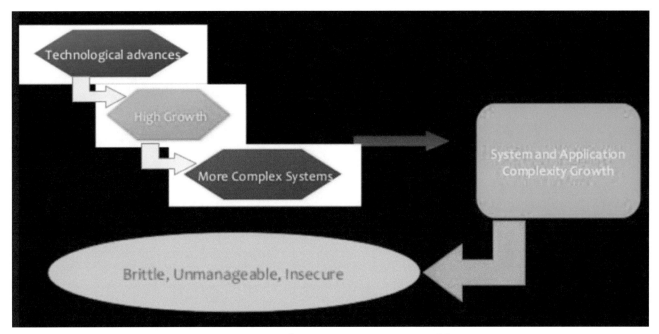

Figure 12.1 Why autonomic computing? [1].

12.2 FUNDAMENTALS OF AUTONOMIC COMPUTING

The term "autonomic" means involuntary or unconscious and refers to the autonomic nervous system. The term "autonomic computing "was introduced in October 2001 by Paul Horn, IBM's senior vice president of research. Since then, IBM has launched their AC unit and integrated AC capabilities into their products. IBM is committed to the vision of promoting AC technologies and working with companies to incorporate the technologies.

Autonomic computing is one of the building blocks of pervasive computing. It is a relatively new discipline inherited from bioinspired computing. The concept of autonomy is inspired by the human autonomic nervous system that controls vital body, handles complexity and uncertainties, and responds automatically to problems (e.g. security threats and system failure) with minimum human intervention. The fundamental building block of an autonomic system is the sensing capability and pro–activeness, i.e. continually seeks ways to improve its performance.

Autonomic computing is emerging as a significant new strategic and holistic approach to the design of computing systems. It envisions the realization of computing systems and applications that are capable of managing themselves without the need for human intervention. It is related to other computer paradigms including grid computing, utility computing, pervasive computing, ubiquitous computing, invisible computing, ambient intelligence, ambient networks, etc. [4].

Autonomic systems are designed to manage growing complexity by making individual system components self-managing. To achieve its purpose, every autonomic system should have the following characteristics [5]: (1) Automatic - being able to self-control its internal functions and operations; (2) Adaptive - being able to change its operation; (3) Aware – being able to control adaptation of its operational behavior. AC system must be active and available 24/7. Today's software applications, which are expected to operate with minimal human oversight, must operate with self-awareness.

IBM researchers introduced the concept of an "autonomic element" (AE) as a fundamental building block for autonomic systems and applications. AEs are intelligent agents and their interactions produce self-managing behavior. A typical architecture for AEs that is shown in Figure 12.2 [6]. Every autonomic element consists of one autonomic manager and one or more managed elements. At the core of an autonomic element is a control loop that integrates the manager with the managed element [7]. The autonomic manager consists of sensors and effectors. It is a controller which controls the managed elements.

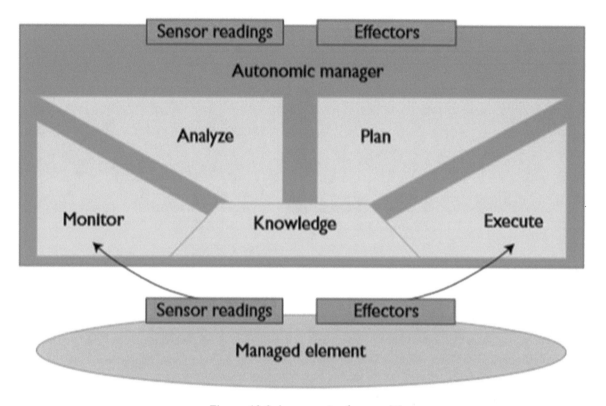

Figure 12.2 Autonomic element [6].

12.3 AUTONOMIC PROPERTIES

For an AC system, IBM defined the following four properties [5,8]:

- *Self-configuration*: Automatically configure and reconfigure itself depending on the changing environment;
- *Self-healing:* Automatic correction of faults or errors, diagnosing and acting to prevent disruptions;
- *Self-optimization*: Automatic monitoring and optimizing its performance to ensure the most efficient computing process;
- *Self-protection:* Proactive identification and protection from arbitrary attacks.

Later, IBM and others (HP, Sun, Microsoft, Intel, etc.) have added more to these basic properties as follows [5]:

- *Self-regulation*: A system that operates to maintain some parameter.
- *Self-learning:* Systems use machine learning techniques without external control.

- *Self-awareness*: A system must know itself, i.e. the extent of its own resources in order to control and manage them.
- *Self-organization*: Realizing self – management of complex IT systems in intended to free system administrators from the details of system operation and maintenance.
- *Self-creation:* A system's members are self-motivated and self-driven.
- *Self-management:* A system that manages or governs itself without external intervention.
- *Self-description:* A system explains itself. It is capable of being understood (by humans) without further explanation.

Some of these properties are illustrated in Figure 12.3 [9]. AC systems are often called self-★ systems (or self-star system), where ★ is a placeholder for the type of behavior. For example, self-managed systems do not require manual updating, and self-healing systems are capable of repairing themselves.

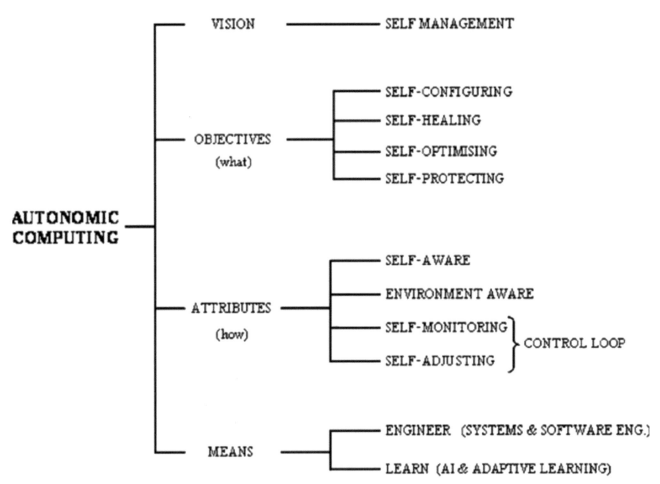

Figure 12.3 Autonomic computing tree [9].

12.4 APPLICATIONS

A typical AC application will involve embedding the complexity in the system infrastructure (hardware and software) and then automating its management. Autonomic computing applications come in two general ways: One resembles feedback-based control and the other resembles self-organized systems found in the biological world (such as cellular automata and neural networks). AC has been applied to e-commerce, e-government, modern software systems, SCADA protection, seamless e-sourcing, grid computing, and dynamic e-business.

- *E-commerce:* AC system can be deployed effectively in e-commerce. E-commerce has created demand for high quality information technology services, and businesses seek ways to improve the quality of service in a cost-effective way.
- *E-government:* E-government (also known as digital government) is a global phenomenon whereby public servants leverage information and communication technology (ICT) to better serve their constituents [10]. It is supposed to improve government and increase citizen satisfaction levels. E-government promises to integrate systems across departments. Integration and interoperability can be realized as AC techniques facilitate communication and operation among systems [11].
- *Smart manufacturing:* Manufacturers are always looking for ways to reduce cost of material, labor, operations, and maintenance. Autonomic smart manufacturing is basically an integrated decision support system that combines process and optimization models in a seamless manner [12].
- *Software Systems:* Database systems have benefited from the AC initiative. Today, software has become ubiquitous and highly complex. Most software used for peer-to-peer (P2P) systems is inherently autonomic because it can handle failures of nodes and network configuration automatically. In the P2P network, each workstation on the network can dynamically serve as client or server and computers can dynamically share services and resources directly with each other. Peer-to-peer systems used for social networking (e.g Facebook) or telephony (e.g. Skype) rely on self-configuration, self-tuning and self-organization [13]. Hadoop provides self-healing and self-organizing features. It is an open-source framework that allows storing and processing big data in a distributed environment. Microsoft Windows XP has an automatic update function [14].
- *SCADA Protection:* The supervisory control and data acquisition (SCADA) systems are used to monitor and control infrastructure such as transportation networks, manufacturing, health facilities, and power grid. AC can be applied to meet the challenges in the cyber threat on SCADA complex systems. The concept of AC provides an advantage over the traditional defense approaches due the self-protecting nature of AC systems [15].
- *NASA:* NASA builds complex mission critical systems using AC-based solutions. Autonomy is important to their mission because it helps develop spacecraft systems that can explore regions in space [16].
- *Autonomic Cloud Computing:* Cloud computing has emerged as a dominant paradigm that provides on-demand access to computing utilities. Autonomic cloud computing emerges as a result of applying four self-management properties of Autonomic Computing (self-configuration, self-healing, self-optimization, and self-protection) in cloud environment. It empowers cloud infrastructures and platforms so that these can take their own decisions to incessantly achieve their assigned jobs [17].
- *Data Center:* Datacenters consume a huge amount of energy, which leads to high operational costs. An autonomic data center will host several applications or services on behalf of multiple customers. The center will determine which resources are needed to satisfy the service-level agreement, automatically provision and configure the appropriate resources accordingly. The data center exhibits several important self-management properties that will characterize all fully autonomic computing systems [18].

- *Smart Grids*: The electric power grid is a complex system consisting of generation sources, transmission system, and distribution network. Smart grid refers to the technology designed to modernize the existing utility grid. It requires extending autonomic computing into the electricity network for energy innovation [19].

Other applications of AC include autonomic personal computing, autonomic laboratory, server load balancing, smart cities, process allocation, monitoring power supply, vehicular ad hoc networks (VANETs), autonomic systems for smart homes, unmanned aerial vehicles (UAVs), autonomous marine vehicles (AMVs), memory error-correction, and automated system backup.

12.5 BENEFITS AND CHALLENGES

Any computing problem that involves large-scale, complex infrastructure will benefit greatly from autonomic computing. Autonomous features will make way into devices and AC will make computers serve you just like the airline, telecom operator, bank, and hotel. The main benefits of AC include fewer personnel, less frequent breakdown, less maintenance cost, time, and less human effort through automation. AC promises to simplify the management of computing systems [20]. This allows IT professionals to focus on higher-value tasks. Despite the benefits, there are still problems and challenges that remain to be solved. Virtually every aspect of AC poses some challenges. These include [21]: the life cycle of an autonomic element; design, test, and verification; installation and configuration; monitoring and problem determination; and need of a common standard. It is very hard to mimic human brain using computers, since the brain consists of a 200 billion neurons that are interconnected by trillions of synapses. Although computing systems have great benefits of speed and automation, there is an urgent need to automate their maintenance such as software updates.

Designing autonomic systems is complex task and poses special challenges. It requires using hard computing and soft computing. It is challenging to build close-loop systems in an open architecture with multiple components from different vendors because components must interoperate seamlessly. Fear of automation replacing your job can discourage administrators from adopting AC. As an emerging field, people know less about AC. More research is required to realize the AC overarching vision [22].

12.6 CONCLUSION

Autonomic computing is the solution to the crisis of coping with the complexity of today's computing systems, which has grown beyond the limits of what system administrators can handle. It refers to computer's ability to manage itself automatically through adaptive technologies. The main objective of autonomic computing is to create systems that manage themselves, while maintaining reliability and keeping the system's complexity invisible to the user. It will minimize the effort of IT personnel and substantially reduce cost. For this reason, the worldwide research community has embraced autonomic computing. Several elements of computing systems have been made more autonomic and introduced to the marketplace.

Autonomic computing has now evolved into a discipline of computer science. It is an amalgamation of techniques from several existing areas including control theory, software engineering, human–computer interaction, machine learning, and artificial intelligence. Its future largely depends on the developments in other technologies that provide an infrastructure for it. Vendors gradually build autonomy into their systems to achieve self-management.

Universities around the world are offering courses on AC. As AC systems mature, they become amazingly complex and will require daunting expertise and patience to get them running. For more information on autonomous computing, one should consult books in [23-27] and the two related journals:

- *International Journal of Autonomic Computing*
- *IEEE Intelligent Systems*

REFERENCES

[1] J. Singh, "Autonomic computing," https://www.slideshare.net/jaspreet93/autonomic-computing-basics-presentation

[2] Y. Wang, "Exploring machine cognition mechanisms for autonomic computing," *International Journal of Cognitive Informatics and Natural Intelligence,* vol. 3, no. 1, January 2009, pp. 1-16.

[3] M. N. O. Sadiku, A. E. Shadare, and S.M. Musa, "Autonomic computing: A primer," *International Journal of Trends in Research and Development,* vol. 5, no. 1, Jan.-Feb. 2018, pp. 357-359.

[4] R. Sterritt, "Autonomic computing," *Innovations System Software Engineering*, vol. 1, 2005, pp. 79–88.

[5] "Autonomic computing," *Wikipedia,* the free encyclopedia https://en.wikipedia.org/wiki/Autonomic_computing

[6] G. Tesauro, "Reinforcement learning in autonomic computing: A manifesto and case studies," *IEEE Internet Computing,* 2007, pp. 22-30.

[7] M. Parashar and S. Hariri, "Autonomic computing: An overview," in J. P. Banˆatre et al. (eds.), *Unconventional Programming Paradigms*. Berlin: Springer-Verlag, 2005, pp. 247–259.

[8] M. C. Huebscher and J. A. McCain, "A survey of autonomic computing—Degrees, models and applications," *ACM Computing Surveys*, vol. 40. No.3, August 2008.

[9] R. Sterritt and D. Bustard, "Autonomic computing—A means of achieving dependability?" *Proceedings of the 10 th IEEE International Conference and Workshop on the Engineering of Computer-Based Systems,* 2003.

[10] M. N. O. Sadiku, A. E. Shadare, S. Koay, and S. M. Musa, "Digital government: A primer," *International Journal of Engineering Research and Advanced Technology*, vol. 2, no. 11, Nov. 2016, pp. 10-13.

[11] S. Furlong, "Applicability of autonomic computing to e-government problems," *Transforming Government: People, Process and Policy,* vol. 2, no. 1, 2008, pp. 8-15.

[12] D. A. Menasce, M. Krishnamoorthy, and A. Brodsky, "Autonomic smart manufacturing," *Journal of Decision Systems,* vol. 24, no. 2, 2015, pp. 206-224.

[13] What is autonomic computing? January 2011, https://sciencenode.org/feature/what-autonomic-computing.php

[14] R. Sterritt and D. F. Bantz, "Personal autonomic computing reflect reactions and self-healing," *IEEE Transaction on Systems, Man, and Cybernetics – Part C: Applications and Reviews*, vol. 36, no. 3, May 2006, pp. 304-314.

[15] S. Nazir, S. Patel, and D. Patel, "Autonomic computing meets SCADA security," *Proceedings of IEEE 16th International Conference of Cognitive Informatics & Cognitive Computing,* July 2017 pp. 498-502.

[16] M. A. Yahya, M. A. Yahya, and A. Dahanayake, "Autonomic computing: A framework to identify autonomy requirements," *Procedia Computer Science*, vol. 20, 2013, pp. 235-241.

[17] P. T. Endo, D. Sadok, and J. Kelner, "Autonomic cloud computing: Giving intelligence to simpleton nodes," *Proceedings of the Third IEEE International Conference on Coud Computing Technology and Science,* 2011, pp. 502-505.

[18] D. A. Menasce and J. O. Kephart, "Autonomic computing," *IEEE Internet Computing*, January/ February 2007, pp. 18-21.

[19] M. Greer and M. Rodriguez-Martinez, "Autonomic computing drives innovation of energy smart grids," *Procedia Computer Science*, vol. 12, 2012, pp. 314 – 319.

[20] "Benefits of autonomic computing," http://hareenlaks.blogspot.com/2011/03/benefits-of-autonomic-computing.html

[21] J. O. Kephart and D. M. Chess, "The vision of autonomic computing," *Computer*, January 2003, pp. 41-50.

[22] F. M. T. Brazier et al., "Agents and service-oriented computing for autonomic computing: A research agenda," *IEEE Internet Computing*, May/June 2009, pp. 82-87.

[23] R. Murch, *Autonomic Computing.* IBM Press, 2004.

[24] M. K. Denko, L. T. Yang, and Y. Zhang, *Autonomic Comuting and Networking.* New York, NY: Springer, 2009.

[25] P. Cong-Vinh (ed.), *Formal and Practical Aspects of Autonomic Computing and Networking: Specification, Development, and Verification.* Information Science Reference, 2002.

[26] P. Lalanda**,** J. A. McCann, and A. Diaconescu**,** *Autonomic Computing: Principles, Design and Implementation.* Springer, 2013.

[27] M. Parashar and S. Hariri**,** *Autonomic Computing: Concepts, Infrastructure, and Applications.* Boca Raton, FL: CRC Press, 2006.

13

ORGANIC COMPUTING

No one can make you feel inferior without
your consent.
- Eleanor Roosevelt

13.1 INTRODUCTION

It has long been observed that computing systems are growing in complexity for developing and maintaining, but human beings dislike complexity. Complex technical systems have become an unavoidable part of life. Such complex systems often consist of a large number of subsystems that interact with one another and with the environment. There is a need for approaches which can effortlessly cope with complexity. The vision of achieving self-management in our complex computing systems has been realized by a proliferation of initiatives such as adaptive infrastructure, proactive computing, self-aware computing, autonomic computing, and organic computing.

Like autonomic computing, organic computing (OC) is an approach to handle the growing system complexity. While autonomic computing is based on the autonomic nervous system, organic computing is based on information processing in biological entities. Organic computing is a type of biologically-inspired computing with organic properties. The field of organic computing aims at translating well-evolved principles of biological systems to engineering complex system design. By organic, we mean systems are capable of autonomously reacting to changes in their environment.

A major concept applicable to autonomic and organic computing are the so-called self-X properties like self-organization, self-configuration, self-optimization, self-healing or self-protection, shown in Figure 13.1 [1]. More specifically [2]:

- *Self-organization* means the system's ability to organize its operation without an external control and to adapt to changes of itself and the environment. It is related to change of structure of system. Some components can leave while others can join according to certain goals.
- *Self-configuration* enables the system to find a working initial configuration. A system is meant to be configured by following high-level policies and adjust the rest of the system automatically.
- *Self-optimization* allows the system to autonomously make best use of the available resources. The system should at all times be optimizing itself with as little manual input as possible.

- *Self-healing* describes the detection of and automatic recovery from failures. A system should to be highly resistant to errors and are supposed to fix any problems in the system by itself. It can correct its errors.
- *Self-protection* enables the system to react properly to attacks. The system protects itself against dangerous environments by adapting to them.
- *Self-adaptation* describes the ability of a system to adapt to a changing environment according to a predefined model. Self-adaptive systems can deal with unforeseeable changes of requirements due to changes of environment or resources during runtime.

This chapter provides a brief introduction to organic computing. It starts by explaining the concept of organic computing and introducing organic computing systems. Then it presents some applications, benefits, and challenges of organic computing. The last section concludes with comments.

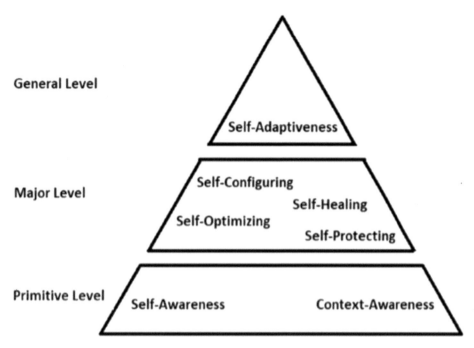

Figure 13.1 Hierarchy of self-X properties [1].

13.2 CONCEPT OF ORGANIC COMPUTING

Computing systems are becoming more and more complex and heterogeneous. Several approaches have been suggested for controlling self-organization process in complex systems. One of those approaches is organic computing, which aims at mastering complexity in technical systems. It is closely related to autonomic computing and exhibits the same properties: self-organizing, self-configuring, self-healing, self-protecting, self-explaining, and context-aware.

The trend in computing community is to make technical systems organic. Organic refers to the systems that are capable of autonomously reacting to changes in their environment. Organic computing proposes new approaches to design organic systems that have the ability to observe their environment and the capabilities to adapt to changing environmental conditions. These systems exhibit the following self-★ properties: self-organising, self-adapting, self-configuring, self-healing, self-protecting, and self-explaining. IBM was the first company to propose a concept for systems implementing these properties.

Thus, organic computing can be regarded as an extension of the autonomic computing vision of IBM. Figure 13.2 shows organic computing is embracing software, neuroscience, and molecular biology [3].

Organic computing has the following five properties: self-awareness, adaptability, trust, approximation, and controlled emergence [4-6].

- *Self-awareness*: It can observe itself and optimize its behavior to meet its goals. To get such behavior, the systems must be aware of their surroundings and their environment. Self-awareness (or introspection) means that the system can observe itself while it is executing.
- *Adaptability*: OC systems are easier to maintain, because they can automatically configure themselves and are more convenient to use because of automatic adaptation to new situations. Adaptation is the ability of the computer to change what if necessary. The computer performs appropriate adaptation to correct errors observed. Self-healing is an important special case of adaptation.
- *Trust*: Trust is relevant in situations that involve a risk on behalf of the trusting individuals. Organic systems must be trustworthy to avoid the risk of losing control. They should adjust to human needs in a trustworthy way. Trust is a multi-dimensional concept that includes safety, reliability, credibility, and usability. Trust is also a measure for predictability of an interaction partner.
- *Approximation:* Approximate computation means that the computer does not always use the most available precision to accomplish a task. It is approximate because it uses the least amount of precision to accomplish a given task. An organic computer can choose automatically between a range of representations to optimize execution.
- *Emergence*: Emergent global behavior is a key aspect of OC systems. Emergent phenomena are often identified when the global behavior of a system appears more coherent and directed than the behavior of individual components of the system.

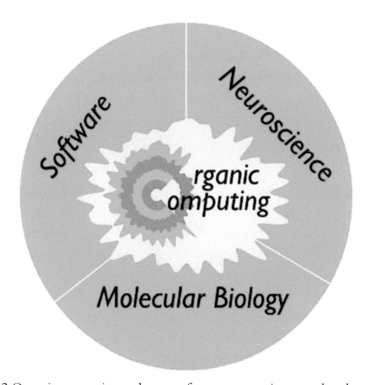

Figure 13.2 Organic computing embraces software, neuroscience, and molecular biology [3].

13.3 ORGANIC SYSTEMS

An organic computing system (or just organic system) typically consists of a large number of autonomous and self-managed entities, where individual entities cooperate to determine the behavior of the entire ensemble system. An "organic computer" is a system that adapts dynamically to the current conditions of its environment. Organic computers are illustrated in Figure 13.3 [7]. Organic computing systems behave life-like and are inspired by biological phenomena or nature. Nature has evolved to cope with scale, complexity, heterogeneity, dynamism, unpredictability, and lack of guarantees. Given a goal and a budget, an organic computer finds the best way to accomplish the goal with the minimal amount of resources and energy.

OC systems are dynamic, consisting of a number of adaptable components and are located in an ever changing environment. To cope with these circumstances, OC systems employ self-organisation mechanisms. Organic systems have been studied for quite some time by mathematicians, sociologists, physicists, economists, systems engineers, and computer scientists. Organic systems, which adapt without human intervention, builds upon other research directions [8]:

- *Machine Learning*: This is an essential property of OC systems. Its goal is to provide solutions which are trained by data or by experience coming from the environment. A machine learning mechanism is needed to fulfill the self-improving property. OC architecture explicitly allows for self learning using artificial neural networks. The learning mechanism in the OC architecture is an integral part of the controller. The goal of machine learning is to provide solutions which are trained by data or experience coming from their operating environment.
- *Optimisation:* The organic computing system optimises the number of tasks finished in a certain time period.
- *Multi Agent Systems*: Organic systems are usually not isolated but work together with other intelligent systems. The systems can be regarded as agents interacting with each other, making the agents social. The agents must be trustworthy and co-operative. The interaction enables the agents to achieve a higher goal which could not be achieved by any of its individual agents. Based on the number of agents, OC system can be classified as [9]: (1) small systems, with just a few agents, (2) middle-size systems, with less than a few hundred agents, (3) large-scale systems, with more than a few hundred agents.
- *Human Machine Interaction:* Multi agent systems interact with humans and an interface is needed. Today, computers are constantly connected and participating in the full breadth of human existence. The development of OC systems that require involvement of human users necessitates a perspective that incorporates different facets of trust.

Social insects, like ants and bees, are a source of inspiration for the design of OC systems.

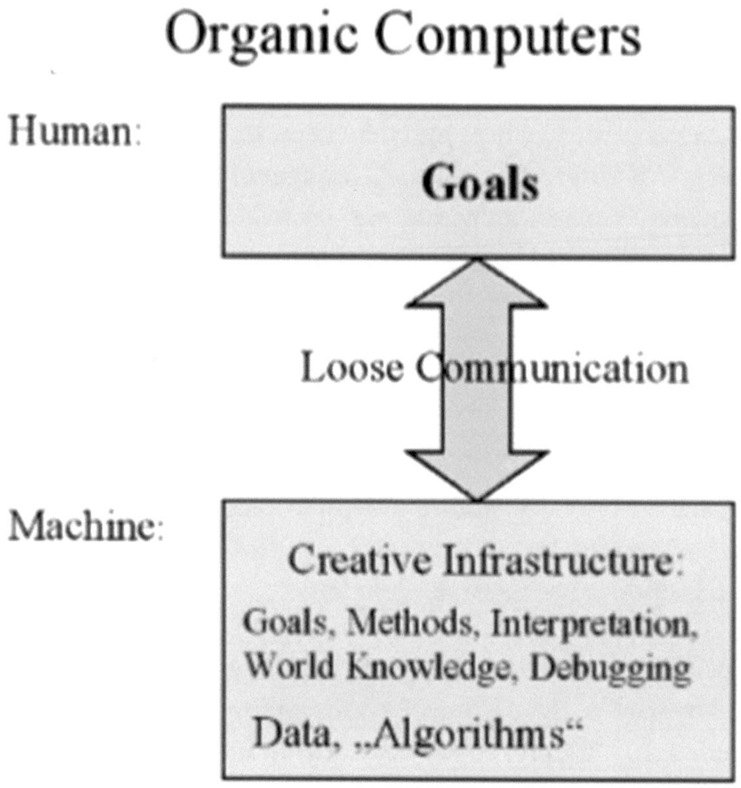

Organic Computers

Human:

Goals

↕ Loose Communication

Machine:

Creative Infrastructure:
Goals, Methods, Interpretation,
World Knowledge, Debugging

Data, „Algorithms"

Figure 13.3 In organic computing, the only task humans hold on to is the setting of goals [3].

13.4 APPLICATIONS

There is a large number of OC application systems, envisioned or already under implementation,. Common applications include the Internet, wireless sensor networks, computer vision, organic systems on chip, information technology, wetware computing, traffic management and control, communication protocols, grid computing, cyber-physical systems, robotics, object recognition, automotive environment, space research, cloud services, mobile cloud computing, smart homes, smart power grid, smart warehouse, smart office building, and smart camera systems [10].

- *Wetware Computer*: A wetware computer is an organic computer composed of organic material such as living neurons. It is also known as an artificial organic brain or a neurocomputer. The brain outperforms the best computers at any task. Although wetware is still largely conceptual, there has been limited success with construction and prototyping. Unlike conventional computer architecture which operates in binary, neurons are capable of existing in thousands of states and communicate with each other through its many synaptic connections. In 1999 William Ditto and his team at Georgia Institute of technology created a basic form of a wetware computer capable of simple addition [11].
- *Robotics*: OC can be used to realize a self-organizing, reliable, adaptive, and robust aerial robotic ensembles that are capable of adjusting to new situations. The approach is limited to single, isolated robots – information exchange with other robots or collaborative efforts among robotic teams were not envisaged in the original design concept. The Robot Operating System (ROS) provides

a high-level software interface for programing and communicating with different kinds of robots [12]. It is not possible to predict the exact positions of the robots. In the future, robots should be autonomous and cost less. Such autonomous robots are used in smart factories.

- *Organic Mobile Cloud Computing:* Mobile devices have become an integral and indispensable part of our life. Mobile cloud computing (MCC) is the new type of cloud computing which utilizes the techniques of cloud computing for the treatment and storage of mobile devices data in the cloud. Organic mobile cloud computing is a system which allows methods to be annotated and offloaded automatically to cloud servers [13].

- *Automotive:* Modern cars are complex systems operating in diverse environments. They consist of dumb and smart components. The dumb/passive components are all parts without electronics, while smart/ active components consist of a wide array of actuators, sensors, and electronic control units (ECUs). Organic computing is an approach to deal with the complexity. Its principles can be used to realize a flexible automation system. It can be used to enhance security and safety of an automotive [14].

- *Online Transfer Learning* (OTL): This is a machine learning concept in which the knowledge gets transferred between the source domain and target domain in real time It can be an efficient method for transferring experiences and data gained from the space analysis to a new learning task. The main advantage of OTL is that it continuously updates the model with new data. Organic computing seeks to master the complexity of a technical system by equipping the system with life-like properties. The combination of OTL with organic computing produces a high result in space for machine learning models, helps to solve new tasks, and learns from new experiences to enhance future capabilities for space programs [15]. It also helps a vehicle learn and assimilate knowledge.

- *Traffic Light Systems*: These systems are a key component of modern cities, where traffic flows are changing constantly. The road networks are characterized by numerous signalized intersections that regulate the traffic flows. To facilitate an efficient flow of traffic and route drivers quickly to their destination demands that traffic light systems are dynamically changing, adaptive, and self-organizing. Traffic light controllers need the ability to adjust quickly to changes in traffic situations. OC principles are being applied to the design of controllers for traffic lights. The Organic Traffic Control (OTC) project develops an adaptive traffic light controller with learning capabilities [16].

- *Smart Camera Systems:* These consist of large numbers of networked cameras which can adjust their fields of view by panning, tilting, and zooming. Smart cameras are cameras with a build-in computation unit that can be utilized for several tasks, such as, image processing, object localization, and object tracking. The performance of a smart camera is strongly influenced by the other neighboring cameras. Due to the increasing number of cameras in these systems manual administration is impossible and there is need for autonomous system. Camera based surveillance systems are used at airports and train stations, for example. Organic computing is driven by the vision of addressing the challenges of complex distributed systems by making them more life-like or organic. Figure 13.4 shows the smart camera system [17].

- *Smart Grid:* Power grid used to be strictly centralized. Internet builds a worldwide heterogeneous parallel computer know as the Grid. With the use of OC, the system has moved to a self organizing, self-configurable, self-healing, and self-optimizing entity.

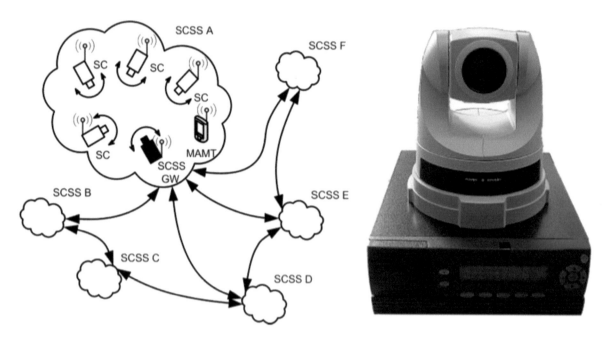

Figure 13.4 .Networked system architecture (left) and smart camera prototype (right) [17].

13.5 BENEFITS

OC has fulfilled the vision of self-organizing technical systems adapting robustly to dynamically changing environments. It promotes complex system design by means of a universal, controller -based concept for self-organizing behavior. The benefit of such systems is that they are dependable and can compensate for some failures. Such systems can maintain themselves and would not need of humans for their operation and maintenance. They should enable future ICT systems to carry out certain tasks on their own. As the systems become increasingly more complex, powerful, and smaller, our environment will be filled with collections of autonomous systems, which are equipped with intelligent sensors and actuators and can communicate and to organize themselves.

An organic computer can be given a goal and a budget; it then finds the best way to accomplish the goal with the minimal amount of resources and energy available. It can achieve 100x improvement in power efficiency and cost performance over extant computers [4].

13.6 CHALLENGES

In spite of the progress in developing OC systems, a number of key challenges still remain. Designing and constructing complex, self-organizing systems for real-world domains is challenging. Due to the complexity it will be impossible to design the behavior of the components for every conceivable situation. The application of OC technology generates severe technical, societal, and political challenges. OC has the problem of their controllability. So far OC is almost exclusively based on strongly simplified artificial models. It is practically impossible to build circuits using only organic materials because one needs to use metals for the interconnects. Due to the steadily increasing complexity, it is hardly possible to design the behavior of each component for every potentially situation. The growing interconnectedness and increasing computational power pose new challenges to designers and users. The performance of the organic computers is so poor that there is no chance in the foreseeable future that they will replace the silicon-based computer chips in current computing devices. The use of self-organization in computing systems may lead to unpredictable global effects. The list of challenges is by no means complete [18].

13.7 CONCLUSION

Adaptivity and self-organization are the main characteristics of future complex computers and computerized systems. Such computer systems will have life-like or "organic" properties. Organic computing is an initiative that has the goal of creating computing systems that are self-organizing, self-configuring, self-healing, self-protecting, and self-explaining. It is building systems inspired by nature. It is one approach to handle the growing system complexity.

Organic computing systems are dynamic, composed of vast number of adaptable components, and located in an ever changing environment. They basically aim to deliver next generation autonomous systems that are expected to cope with situations that have not been modeled before. Emergent global behavior is a key feature of OC systems.

As an idea whose time simply has come, organic computing is thriving from multiple roots. Organic computer based on organic mediums such as DNA (as alternatives to silicon) can redefine what a computer is and change everything. The trend in computer science is to design and build organic systems as next generation systems that can cope with ever-increasing complexity. More information on organic computing can be found in books in [7,10,19-21].

REFERENCES

[1]   A. Niederquell, "Self-adaptive systems in organic computing: Different concepts of self-improvement," https://arxiv.org/pdf/1808.03519.pdf

[2]   U. Brinkschulte, "Model-driven design and organic computing – Contradictory or synergetic approaches to overcome the embedded software crisis," *Proceedings of IEEE International Symposium on Object/Component/Service-Oriented Real-Time Distributed Computing,* 2009, pp. 91-92.

[3]   N. Matsumaru et al., "Chemical organization theory as a theoretical base for chemical computing," *International Journal of Unconventional Computing,* vol. 3, no. 4, 2007, pp. 285-309.

[4]   M. N. O. Sadiku, P. O. Adebo, S.M. Musa, and O. D. Olaleye, "Organic computing," *International Journals of Advanced Research in Computer Science and Software Engineering,* vol. 9, no. 7, July 2019, pp.1-4.

[5]   A. Agarwal and B. Harrod, "Organic computing," August 2006, https://www.scribd.com/document/101280696/Agarwal-Harrod-Organic-2006

[6]   J. P. Steghofer et al., "Trustworthy organic computing systems: Challenges and perspectives,: in B. Xie et al. (eds.), *Autonomic and Trusted Computing. Lecture Notes in Computer Science,* vol 6407. Springer, Berlin, Heidelberg, 2010, pp. 62-76.

[7]   R. P. Wurtz (ed.), *Organic Computing.* Berlin, Germany: Springer-Verlag, 2008, p. 11.

[8]   M. Sommer, "Organic computing fundamentals – Learning from nature," http://www.matthiassommer.it/organic-computing/organic-computing-learning-from-nature/

[9]   N. M. Sasankan, "Mutual influences in interwoven systems and their detection in the context of organic computing," July 2018, https://arxiv.org/pdf/1807.08262.pdf

[10] C. Muller-Schloer, H. Schmeck, and T. Ungerer (eds.), *Organic Computing: A Paradigm Shift for Complex Systems.* Springer, 2011.

[11] "Wetware computing," *Wikipedia*, the free encyclopedia https://en.wikipedia.org/wiki/Wetware_computer

[12] S. von Mannen, S. Tomforde, and J. Hahner, "An organic computing approach to self-organizing robot ensembles," *Frontiers in Robotics and AI*, November 2016.

[13] S. Nadouri and H. Fellah, "OMCC: Organic mobile cloud computing," *Proceedings of the 8th International Conference on Modelling, Identification and Control*, Algiers, November 2016, pp. 169-173.

[14] K. Lamshöft, R. Altschaffel, and J. Dittmann, "Adapting organic computing architectures to an automotive environment to increase safety & security," in P Dencker et al. (eds.), *Automotive - Safety & Security,* 2017, pp. 103-119.

[15] S. Natarajan, "Online transfer learning and organic computing for deep space research and astronomy," March 2019, https://doi.org/10.7287/peerj.preprints.27581v1

[16] D. Merkle, M. Middendorf, and A. Scheidler, "Organic computing and swarm intelligence,:" in C. Blum and D. Merkle (eds.), *Swarm Intelligence: Introduction and Applications.* Berlin: Springer-Verlag, 2008, pp. 253-281.

[17] M. Hoffmann, J. Hahner, and C. Muller-Schloer, "Towards self-organising smart camera systems," in U. Brinkschulte et al. (eds.), *Architecture of Computing Systems – ARCS 2008.* Berlin, Germany: Springer-Verlag Berlin, 2008, pp. 220-231.

[18] H. Schmeck, "Organic computing – A new vision for distributed embedded systems," *Proceedings of the Eighth IEEE International Symposium on Object-Oriented Real-Time Distributed Computing,* 2005.

[19] C. Muller-Schloer and S. Tomforde, *Organic Computing – Technical Systems for Survival in the Real World.* Springer, 2017.

[20] S. Tomforde and B. Sick (eds*.), Organic Computing: Doctoral Dissertation Colloquim 2016.* Kassel University Press, 2017.

[21] M. Gutmann, M. Decker, and J. Knifka (eds*.), Evolutionary Robotics, Organic Computing and Adaptive Ambience : Epistemological and Ethical Implications of Technomorphic Descriptions of Technologies.* Hermeneutics and Anthropology, vol. 6, 2015.

14

STOCHASTIC COMPUTING

He who loses wealth loses much; he who loses a friend loses more; but he who loses courage loses all.
- Anonymous

14.1 INTRODUCTION

The continuing ability of manufacturers to produce smaller devices with each technology generation has resulted in exponentially increasing circuit density. The manufacturing challenges that accompany technology scaling has led to uncertainty in performance and reliability that threaten the continuation of Moore's law. As variability in circuit behavior increases, traditional approaches that aim to enforce deterministic behavior on a non-deterministic substrate become increasingly expensive [1]. As semiconductor technology approaches the deep nanoscale regime, the stochasticity of the device and circuit fabric will need to be addressed. There is a need for unconventional computing methods that directly address these issues. A new vision for stochastic computing has begun to emerge as the solution. Designers have now started to embrace stochasticity at many layers of the computing stack.

Stochastic computing (SC) or probabilistic computing was proposed in the 1960s as a low-cost alternative to conventional binary computing, but recently has received increasing attention from academia. It performs operations using probability instead of arithmetic. Its operations converts a fairly complicated computation into a series of very simple operations on random bits. Although the stochastic computer has similarities to both analog and digital computers, it is radically different from both. It is uniquely different in that it represents and processes information in the form of digitized probabilities.

This chapter introduces stochastic computing. It starts with presenting the basics of stochastic computing and stochastic logic circuits. Then it discusses SC applications, benefits, and challenges. The last section concludes with some comments.

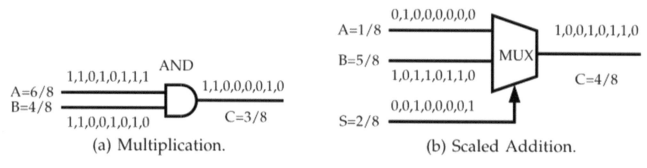

(a) Multiplication.   (b) Scaled Addition.

Figure 14.1 Stochastic implementation of arithmetic operations [4].

14.2 STOCHASTIC COMPUTING BASICS

Stochastic computing (SC) refers to the method of using probabilistic representations of numbers to perform numerical operations. Stochastic computing can provide compact, error-tolerant and low-power implementations of complex functions. It was introduced in 1953 by John von Neumann. He addressed the problem of reliable computation in the presence of unreliable components. Active research on stochastic computing dwindled over the next few years due to the fact it could not compete with more traditional digital logic. As a computing paradigm, SC is currently undergoing a revival. Since stochastic circuits has small size, SC has regained interest recently due to its potential usage in some emerging nanotechnologies. Although stochastic computing was a historical failure, it has shown promise in several applications and still remains relevant for solving certain problems [2].

Stochastic computing is a new alternative approach to conventional real arithmetic. It is an unconventional computing technique originally proposed to reduce the size of digital arithmetic circuit. It can provide compact, error-tolerant, low cost, and low-power implementations of complex problems. Unlike deterministic computing, stochastic computing does not assume that hardware always produces the same results if given the same inputs. It may be viewed as an interpretation of calculations in probabilistic terms since it represents and processes information in the form of digitized probabilities. It allows for noise and uncertainty, and tolerate transient errors in input data. It is a move in the direction of processing by parallel structures similar to those of the human brain. It allows for extremely low cost and low power implementations of common arithmetic operations.

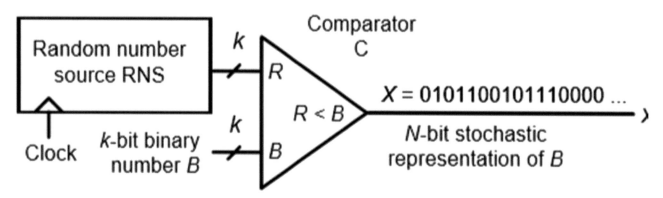

Figure 14.2. Bit stream generation using comparator and random number generator [5].

14.3 STOCHASTIC LOGIC CIRCUITS

Just like binary computers, stochastic circuits process data serially in the form of bit-streams. Stochastic computing may be regarded as a low-cost alternative to conventional binary computing. It is the result of applying probabilistic laws to digital logic systems. To understand SC, it is necessary to understand stochastic representation of data. In the binary representation of numbers, a set of number of bits is used to represent each number. Stochastic numbers are treated as probabilities. Stochastic computing (SC) essentially represents numbers as streams of random bits and reconstructs numbers by calculating frequencies. It performs serial data processing with binomially distributed bit streams. Each stream represents a probability value, obtained as the number of 1 valued bits over the total number of bits. For example, the 10-bit stream "0111001000" represent a real-valued number 0.4. Note that each bit has a probability 0.4 of being one and probability 0.6 of being zero. Thus, we can use the total number of ones in this bit stream to evaluate the real-valued number [3]. The key idea of stochastic computing is to represent a number x with a stream of binary random bits, where x and (1-x) represent the probability of observing '1' and '0' in this stream, respectively. SC employs random bits to calculate via simpler circuits and with greater tolerance for errors. Stochastic logic performs computation on data represented by random bit streams. For example, stochastic multiplication can be performed with a single AND gate and scaled addition can be performed with a single multiplexer unit, as shown in Figure 14.1 [4]. To convert any number into a stochastic bit stream, a comparator and a Random Number Generator (RNG) can be used as shown in Figure 14.2 [5].

Binary encoding systems operate on a positional representation of data. In SC, the signal value is encoded by the probability of obtaining a one versus a zero. The stochastic computer achieves distributed computation through its peculiar representation of data by the probability that a logic level will be ON or OFF at a clock pulse. It is often necessary in stochastic computations to convert inputs from a number style to stochastic form. This requires stochastic number generators (SNGs), which tend to be the most expensive SC components.

Circuits that convert binary numbers to stochastic numbers or vice versa are very basic to SC. A typical stochastic circuit realization of an arithmetic function is shown in Figure 12.3 [6]. This figure needs up to four SNGs for its four inputs. In SC, stochastic numbers are treated as probabilities and they fall naturally into the interval [0,1]. The value of a bitstream is encoded by the number of constituenst 1s and 0s and SC arithmetic circuits operate on the bitstreams. Many operations in SC do not yield exact results.

Conventional digital circuits require thousands of transistors to execute arithmetic operation, while SC performs mathematical manipulations using little power [7]. SC typically involves substantially fewer hardware resources than conventional computing while performing the same algorithm.

SC is known for having a high degree of error tolerance, especially for transient or soft errors caused by process variations. Predictability and error control are prerequisites for any practical computer architecture. A nanoscale memristor is an inherently stochastic device, and extra energy and latency are required to make a deterministic memory based on memristors. This native stochastic computing system can be implemented as a hybrid integration of memristor memory and simple CMOS stochastic computing circuits [8]

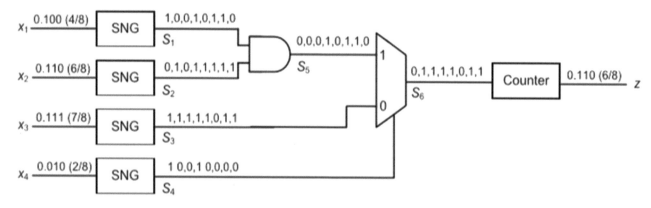

Figure 12.3 Stochastic circuit realizing the arithmetic function [6]: z=x1x2x4 +x3(1−x4)

14.4 APPLICATIONS

What was holding stochastic computing back was the lack of suitable devices to make it practical. There was no hardware available which would make construction of the complex computing structure required in SC.

Although stochastic computing has a number of defects, there are certain applications that highlight its strengths. Stochastic computing techniques have been proposed at nearly all levels of the computing stack. It has been recognized that SC is potentially useful in specialized systems, where small size, low power, or soft-error tolerance are required, and limited precision or speed are acceptable.

Stochastic computing has been investigated for a variety of applications such as addition, multiplication, division, and square-rooting. It has also been applied in artificial neural networks, control machine, machine learning, image processing, and vector quantization. New applications have been in energy, security, digital IIR filters, and medicine.

14.5 BENEFITS AND CHALLENGES.

The major attraction of stochastic computing when it was first introduced in the 1960s is that it enables very low-cost implementations of arithmetic operations using standard logic elements. Stochastic computing systems require fewer logic gates and are well suited for nanoscale CMOS technologies.

One of the main advantages of stochastic computing is its inherent error-tolerance and extremely low-cost of arithmetic units [6]. If one bit becomes flipped, the effect is negligible in a sufficiently long bitstream. This becomes important when electronic devices are scaled down to the point where errors become more frequent. SC provides a rough estimate very rapidly. It is robust against noise; a minor error has no significant impact on the outcome. Stochastic computing elements can tolerate skew in the arrival time of the inputs and consume low power. Besides saving power, SC enables progressive precision, i.e. the precision of the calculations depends on the length of the bitstream used. Making computers efficient at dealing with probabilities at scale is central to our ability to transform current systems into intelligent partners for decision-making. The small size of stochastic components means that they have relatively low power needs.

In spite of these benefits and its inherent error tolerance, SC has some drawbacks. SC was seen as impractical because of long computation time and relatively low accuracy. It also require many stochastic number generators to produce stochastic numbers. A stochastic representation is exponentially longer than conventional binary radix. One major issue of SC is that applications implemented with this technique are limited by the available computational elements. Tradeoffs between precision and memory can be very challenging. By nature, stochastic computing is random. SC requires a means of generating random biased using pseudo-random number generators, which can be expensive. These major challenges must be addressed if the full potential of SC is to be realized.

14.6 CONCLUSION

Stochastic computing is a (re-)emerging computing technique that promises high density, low power, and error tolerant solutions. It is an unconventional method of computation that treats data as probabilities. It has considerable theoretical appeal as a very unconventional way to compute. It has recently regained significant attention due to its fault-tolerance property.

The main performance measures of a computer include physical size, range of possible problems, speed and accuracy of solution, reliability and cost of the computer. In this regard, it is expedient to trade the accuracy of the digital computer and the speed of the analog computer, for the economy of the stochastic computer [9]. One would expect that research in stochastic/probabilistic computing will lead to significant improvement in the reliability, security, serviceability, and performance of AI systems. More information on SC can be found in the books in [10-11].

REFERENCES

[1] J. Sartori and R. Kumar, "Stochastic Computing," *Foundations and Trends in Electronic Design Automation*, vol. 5. no. 3, 2011, pp 153-210.

[2] "Stochastic computing," *Wikipedia,* the free encyclopedia
https://en.wikipedia.org/wiki/Stochastic_computing

[3] P. Li, Analysis, "Design, and logic synthesis of finite-state machine-based stochastic computing," *Doctoral Dissertation*, The University of Minnesota, June, 2013.

[4] M. Alawad and M. Lin, "Survey of stochastic-based computation paradigms," *IEEE Transactions on Emerging Topics in Computing,* vol. 7, no. 1, Jan.-March, 2019, pp. 98 – 114.

[5] A. Alaghi, W. Qian, and J. P. Hayes, "The promise and challenge of stochastic computing," *IEEE Transactions on Computer-Aided Design of Integrated Circuits and Systems*, vol. 37, no. 8, Nov. 2017, pp. 1515-1531.

[6] M. N. O. Sadiku, E. Awada, and S. M. Musa, "Stochastic computing: An introduction," *European Journal of Electrical and Computer Engineering*, vol. 3, no. 6, December 2019.

[7] A. Alaghi and J. P. Hayes, "Computing with randomness," *IEEE Spectrum,* March 2018, pp. 44-51.

[8] P. Knag, W. Lu, and Z. Zhang. "A native stochastic computing architecture enabled by memristors," *IEEE Transactions on Nanotechnology*, vol. 13, no. 2, March 2014, pp. 283 – 293.

[9] B. R. Gaines, "Stochastic computing systems," *Advances in Information System Science*, chapter 2, 1969, pp. 37-172.

[10] W. J. Gross and V. C. Gaudet (eds.), *Stochastic Computing: Techniques and Applications.* Springer, 2019.

[11] J. Sartori and R. Kumar, *Stochastic Computing (Foundations and Trends(r) in Electronic Design Automation).* Hanover, MA: Now Publishers, 2011.

15
CHAPTER

COGNITIVE COMPUTING

Creativity is inventing, experimenting,
growing, taking risks, breaking rules, making
mistakes, and having fun.
- Mary Lou Cook

15.1 INTRODUCTION

Some regard cognitive computing as the third era of computing. In the first era, (19th century) Charles Babbage introduced the concept of a programmable computer. The second era (1950) experienced digital programming computers such as ENIAC and ushered an era of modern computing and programmable systems. Now cognitive computing mimics after the central nervous system of humans. It may also be viewed as a revolution in thinking models since it will bring about a digital disruption.

Like the brain, a cognitive system is an intelligent self-adjustable network consisting of elements that have the ability to learn. It provides digital solutions to meet human-centric requirements: act, think, and behave like a human. It mimics the ability of humans to learn and improve from experience. It is basically a new computing paradigm for solving real world problems. It has been recognized as a key enabling technology for turning big data into insights. It will have far-reaching effects on our private lives, healthcare, business, and more.

Cognitive computing (CC) refers to hardware and/or software that mimics the way the human brain works. It involves self-learning systems that use data mining, pattern recognition, and machine learning algorithms to mimic the functioning of the human brain. Cognitive computing systems are adaptive in that they can learn as information and requirement change. They can resolve ambiguity and tolerate unpredictability. The goal of cognitive computing is to create systems that are capable of solving problems without human intervention [1]. In other words, CC endows computer systems with the faculties of knowing, thinking, and feeling. We will be directly interacting with cognitive systems on a daily basis

This chapter provides an introduction to cognitive computing. It begins by presenting the basics of cognitive computing and cognitive computing systems. It covers the main technologies behind cognitive computing. It presents some applications, benefits, and challenges of CC. The last section concludes with some comments.

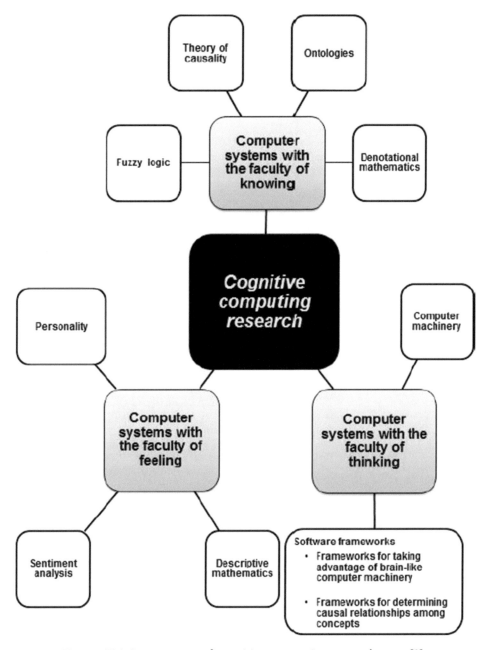

Figure 15.1 A taxonomy of cognitive computing research areas [2].

15.2 BASICS OF COGNITIVE COMPUTING

Cognitive computing differs from traditional computing in that it handles human kinds of problems such as face recognition, speech understanding, medical diagnosis, risk assessment, fraud detection, and sentiment analysis. Such problems are challenging and almost intractable for traditional computing techniques. The relationship between CC and other related areas is shown in Figure 15.1 [2].

Although the term "*cognitive computing*" is often used interchangeably with artificial intelligence, these terms are distinctive. AI and CC remain closely similar in the intent, but they differ in their tendencies to interact naturally with humans. Artificial intelligence (AI) has been described as technologies capable of performing tasks normally requiring human intelligence. Cognitive computing seeks to overcome the boundaries of conventional programmable (von Neumann) computers. Watson, IBM's first cognitive system, demonstrated through a Jeopardy exhibition match that it was capable of answering complex questions as effectively as the world's human champions. In February 2011, Watson defeated Ken Jennings and Brad Rutter at Jeopardy! [3,4]. Watson has been configured to support life sciences research. The modified versions of Watson include medical literature, patents, genomics, and pharmacological data.

15.3 FEATURES OF COGNITIVE SYSTEMS

Cognitive computing systems are designed for cognitive and perceptive knowledge processing. They create solutions for day-to-day problems. The design of such systems brings together researchers from the fields of computer science, psychology, linguistics, philosophy, and neurocomputing. In order of SC to solve the types of problems that humans are typically tasked, cognitive computing systems must have five key attributes, as listed by the Cognitive Computing Consortium [1].

- *Adaptive:* Cognitive systems may learn as information changes and requirements evolve. Cognitive systems can use machine learning to adapt to different contexts with minimal human supervision
- *Interactive:* Human-computer interaction (HCI) is a critical component in cognitive systems. The systems may interact easily with users, processors, devices, and cloud services. Cognitive systems are easier to interact with because they present information in more human terms.
- *Iterative and Stateful:* They may aid in defining a problem by asking questions and they may "remember" previous interactions in a process. Being stateful means that the computer or program keeps track of the state of interaction.
- *Contextual:* They may understand, identify, and extract contextual elements such as meaning, syntax, time, location, process, and regulations. They may draw on multiple sources of information, including structured and unstructured data. Cognitive computing systems make context computable.

15.4 MODELING COGNITION

Using self-learning algorithms that use data mining, pattern recognition and natural language processing, the computer can mimic how the human brain functions. Cognitive computing overlaps with AI and involves many of the same underlying technologies including expert systems, neural networks, machine learning, deep neural networks, natural language processing, robotics, and virtual reality.

There are three main technologies behind cognitive computing. Here is how each of these help in implementing CC [5]:

- *Big Data Analysis*: Big Data has become both a threat and an advantage with many companies. But what do companies do with all this data they collect? Analysis of data by humans can be a time-consuming activity. The main challenge lies in harnessing volumes of data, integrating the data from several sources, and understanding their various formats. New technologies such as cognitive computing offer promise for addressing this challenge. Cognitive systems can be used to crunch this enormous amount of data, which can be both organized and unorganized. Cognitive computing works based on volumes of data, which offers the guarantee of unlocking novel insights and data-driven decisions [6].

- *Machine Learning*: This involves the use of algorithms to enable computers to analyze data and make predictions. Learning is the core of the cognitive system. It gives the functional elements the capability to execute various actions depending on past experiences. In case of cognitive computing, the algorithm needs to be coded to learn on its own. Machine learning is applied to improve the accuracy of the models and make better predictions.
- *Cloud Computing:* Cloud computing refers to delivery of on-demand services, usually through the Internet, on a pay-per-use basis. To analyze huge amount of data requires having extensive computing power. It is viable to opt for these cloud solutions. They provide scalable computing for analyzing data and working on resource-intensive tasks, making them ideal for working on cognitive computing models.

15.5 APPLICATIONS

The aim of cognitive computing is to build applications which model and mimic human thinking. It employs the computing theories, methods, and tools to model human cognition. It can be applied across just about every major industry that relies on data-driven decision-making to improve outcomes. CC applications utilize tools such as natural language processing, image recognition, intelligent search, and decision analysis to adapt their underlying computational algorithms. As cognitive computing platforms become commercially available, real-world applications are starting to emerge. Examples of such real-world applications include the following:

- *Enterprise:* Cognitive systems empower the IT infrastructure of an enterprise. Enterprises use CC applications to pursue one of three distinct business objectives: driving operational excellence, delighting customers, or creating a superior experience for employees. They may use CC technologies to automate business processes, streamline contract analysis, and communicate with customers. Some applications strengthen customer loyalty and trust [7]. Fraud detection is an application of cognitive computing in finance. Its goal is to identify transactions which do not seem to be normal.
- *Healthcare:* The greatest disruption resulting from the rise of cognitive computing will likely occur in the field of healthcare, which is being disrupted and transformed by an exponential growth in data. Cognitive computing enables researchers to uncover relationships among genes, proteins, and diseases. Watson may be applied in a healthcare setting to help collate the span of knowledge about the individual patient's present history, analyze vast quantity of information, and provide a recommendation. This is not to replace the doctor, but to help process the humongous amount of data and make accurate decisions. IBM and other companies are developing various cognitive computing tools for gaining insight into various aspects of health care information. Ultimately, the application of cognitive computing in healthcare is producing superior, best-practice, decision-relevant information for everyone [8].
- *Astronomy:* Astronomers have the unique opportunity to adopt new technologies and methodologies because the impact can be profound and highly beneficial to effecting rapid progress in the field. Projects like DOME are important vehicles for ensuring engagement of the astronomy community with cognitive systems [9].

- *Education:* Human interaction between student and teacher may cause anxiety. With the aid of cognitive computer tutors, students can gain the confidence to learn and do well in the classroom. This cognitive system will not take the place of teachers. The IBM Watson cognitive system has been used to teach parallel programming since the system is capable to learn through user's input and be taught by experts. The system enables a dialog-based interaction with programmers during program development [10]. With cognitive systems, it is feasible to establish personalized and customized teaching and learning environments. Cognitive computing intends to shape the future of higher education.
- *Information security:* Information is the source of knowledge for human beings to know and transform the world. In the real world, the expression of things and information is often inaccurate and uncertain. Cognitive computing applied to information security enables faster, more reliable detection of fraud or other activities. Its ability to work 24/7 makes it suitable for security operations [11].
- *Robotic:* This uses cognitive automation to automate repeatable tasks and improve efficiency, quality, and accuracy.

Other applications include fraud detection in business/finance, investment risk management, astronomy, commerce recommender systems, predictive maintenance in manufacturing, information management, and sign language.

15.6 BENEFITS

The main objective of cognitive computing models is to implement computational intelligence in computer systems, i.e. endow them with the faculties of knowing, thinking, and feeling. In cognitive computing, we expect the system to learn autonomously, without human assistance. It removes humans from the loop and is completely automated. Some key benefits of cognitive computing are as follows [12]:

1. *Better data analysis:* For example, in healthcare industry. cognitive computing will not replace the doctor. It can collate information, reports, and data from disparate sources, and make recommendation.
2. *Efficient processes:* A complex process can be made simpler by employing cognitive computing. CC may be regarded as a collection of algorithmic capabilities that can augment employee performance and automate increasingly complex workloads.
3. *Better level of customer interactions:* CC can provide amazingly relevant, contextual, and accurate information on broad subjects. Cognitive systems are easier to interact with because they present information in more human terms: in language, images, and visual representations.

These advantages highlight the massive potential that cognitive computing possesses. The investment on commercializing cognitive technologies has increased, making them easier to buy and deploy. Cognitive systems are helping people expand their knowledge base, improve their productivity, and deepen their expertise. Cognitive computing is an indispensable technology to develop human–centered smart systems which provide services with higher quality, such as smart healthcare, affective interaction, and autonomous driving.

15.7 CHALLENGES

Some CC applications critically and completely depend on massive amounts of data. There are three challenges concerning data. The first is identifying the right data. The second challenge is ensuring that needed data is available. The third challenge is getting the data into the right format [7].

When developing large-scale simulations with cognitive capacities, some researchers believe that the main challenge lies in improving the realism of the simulations. They believe that simulations should incorporate as much biological detail as possible. In other words, if you use biological brains as templates for designing cognitive computing system, then you should take account of as much biological detail as possible [13]. It is challenging to build a general purpose systems that can learn, reason, and interact in a human natural way. Deciding which aspects of a business process are routine enough to be handed over to the machine and which aspects need to be retained by human users is often difficult. A loss of jobs will be felt across industries as some positions are replaced by machines. Smaller companies who may fall out of the market because they will not have funds to adopt CC. Organizations face the challenge of ongoing supervision of some CC applications. There appears to be a continuum of tasks of increasing difficulty in this area.

15.8 CONCLUSIONS

Cognitive computing can be regarded as the computer simulation of the human reasoning processes. It is an emerging multidisciplinary field of research that links together neurobiology, cognitive psychology, computer science, big data, and artificial intelligence. The idea behind cognitive computing seeks to develop systems that emulate human brain functions such as perception, knowledge accumulation, goal planning, experience, and logical inference. Cognitive systems learn from data, reason from models, and interact with us to perform complex tasks better than humans. Recent advances in data science and computing disciplines (including artificial intelligence, IoT technologies, big data, machine learning, cloud computing, and natural language) are accelerating advances in cognitive computing. With time every digital system will be measured on its cognitive abilities.

The cognitive computing marketing is dominated by large industries like IBM, Microsoft, and Google. For more than seven decades, IBM Research (www.ibm.com/research) has defined the future of information technology. It is the leading company in the field of cognitive computing. Today, IBM is collaborating with more than 250 universities worldwide to help teach various courses on cognitive computing. More information on CC can be found in the books in [14-18].

REFERENCES

[1]   "Cognitive computing," *Wikipedia*, the free encyclopedia, https://en.wikipedia.org/wiki/Cognitive_computing

[2]   J. O. Gutierrez-Garcia and E.lLópez-Neri, "Cognitive computing: A brief survey and open research challenges," *Proceedings of the 3rd International Conference on Applied Computing and Information Technology/2nd International Conferenceon Computational Science and Intelligence*, 2015, pp. 328-333.

[3]   A. Soffer, D. Konopnicki, and H. Roitman, "When Watson went to work - Leveraging cognitive computing in the real world," *Proceedings of the 39th International ACM SIGIR conference,* July 2016, pp. 455-456.

[4]   S. Shostak, "Smart machines: IBM's Watson and the era of cognitive computing," *The European Legacy,* vol. 21, no. 8, 2016, pp. 870-871.

[5]   "What is cognitive computing? 5 Ways to make your business more intelligent," October 2017, https://www.newgenapps.com/blog/what-is-cognitive-computing-applications-companies-artificial-intelligence

[6]   H. Reynolds, "Big data and cognitive computing–Part 1," KMWorld, Jan. 2016, pp. 6-7.

[7]   M. Tarafdar, C. M. Beath, and J. W. Ross,"Enterprise cognitive computing applications: Opportunities and challenges," *IT Professional,* vol. 19, no. 4, 2017, pp.2-27.

[8]   M. N. O. Sadiku, J. Foreman, and S. M. Musa, "Cognitive Computing," *International Journal of Scientific Engineering and Technology*, vol. 7, no. 8, August 2018, pp. 74-75.

[9]   M A Garrett, "Big data analytics and cognitive computing – Future opportunities for astronomical research," *IOP Conference Series: Materials Science and Engineering*, vol. 67, 2014, pp. 1-4.

[10]   A. C. Chozas, S. Memeti, and S. Pllana, "Using cognitive computing for learning parallel programming: An IBM Watson solution," *Procedia Computer Science*, vol. 108C, 2017, pp. 2121–2130.

[11]   G. Finch, B. Goehring, and A. Marshall, "The enticing promise of cognitive computing: high-value functional efficiencies and innovative enterprise capabilities," *Strategy & Leadership*, vol. 45, no. 6, 2017, pp. 26-33.

[12]   "3 Advantages of cognitive computing," October 2017, https://www.goodworklabs.com/cognitive-computing-advantages/ Posted by editor_goodworks on Oct 10, 2017

[13]   M. Colombo, "Why build a virtual brain? Large-scale neural simulations as jump start for cognitive computing," *Journal of Experimental & Theoretical ArtificialIntelligence*, vol. 29, no. 2, 2017, pp. 361-370.

[14]   J. Hurwitz, M. Kaufman, and A. Bowles (eds.), *Cognitive Computing and Big Data Analytics.* Indianapolis, IN: John Wiley & Sons, 2015.

[15]   J. E. Kelly III and S. Hamm, *Smart Machines: IBM's Watson and the Era of Cognitive Computing.* Columbia University Press, 2013.

[16]   V. V. Raghavan et al., *Cognitive Computing: Theory and Applications.* North Holland, 2016.

[17]   A. Masood and A. Hashmi, *Cognitive Computing Recipes : Artificial Intelligence Solutions Using Microsoft Cognitive Services and Tensorflow.* Apress, 2019.

[18]   P. K. Mallick and S. Borah, *Emerging Trends and Applications in Cognitive Computing.* IGI Global, 2019.

16

AFFECTIVE COMPUTING

To avoid criticism, do nothing, say nothing,
be nothing.
- Elbert Hubbard

16.1 INTRODUCTION

The ability of machines to recognize, interpret, and respond according to human emotions is known as affective computing. Affective computing (or emotional computing) derives its name from psychology, in which "affect" is a synonym for "emotion." Emotions (or human affect or feelings) are widely known to affect human decision-making. In spite of the fact that emotion is a fundamental aspect of our daily life, it has been largely ignored by technology over the years partly because it seemed difficult to quantify. The idea of affective computing was first put forward by Professor Rosalind Picard (a computer scientist and IEEE fellow) in 1995 who was in Massachusetts Institute of Technology (MIT) Laboratory [1, 2]. Affective computing combines engineering and computer science with psychology, cognitive science, and sociology.

According to Rosalind Picard, if we want computers to interact naturally with us, we must give them the ability to recognize and express emotions. It is difficult to build a truly intelligent computer without having emotional capabilities like humans do. The basic goal of affective computing is to use affective communication found in human–human interaction and apply it to human–computer interaction. Facial expressions, posture, gestures, tone of voice, and speech can all signify changes in human emotional state, and these can all be detected and used to register changes in human emotional state.

Affective computing (AC) (also known as artificial emotional intelligence) is computing that relates to emotion or other affective phenomena. It explores how technology can inform an understanding of human affect and how interactions between humans and technologies can be impacted by affect. It involves the study and development of systems and devices that can recognize and express human affects or emotions. It uses both hardware and software technology to detect the affective state of a person. It deals with the design of computational devices that exhibit innate emotional capabilities [3].

This chapter provides an introduction to affective computing. It begins by addressing the basics of affective computing. Then it presents some applications, benefits, and challenges of AC. The final chapter concludes with some comments.

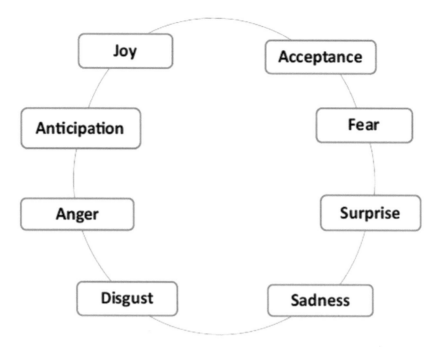

Figure 16.1 Plutchik's emotion wheel [4].

16.2 AFFECTIVE COMPUTING BASICS

Although technologists have largely ignored emotion, emotion is a fundamental part of the human experience or human interactions, influencing everyday tasks such as learning, communication, and decision-making. Emotions influence the very mechanisms of rational thinking, have strong influences on our mentalities, and may affect our physical health. They are universal expressions. For example, facial expressions of emotion are universal, not culturally determined. Emotions play an important role in successful and effective human–human communication. They tell humans what to pay attention to and what to ignore. The six basic emotions are anger, disgust, fear, happiness, sadness, and surprise. This list is by no means exhaustive. Plutchik emotions list, shown in Figure 16.1, is the most common used classification in affective computing [4].

Affective computing (AC) is computing that relates to or influences emotion or other affective phenomena. It is an area that concerned with gathering cues or data about a user's emotional state from a variety of sources, including facial expressions, muscle tension, posture, gestures, speech patterns, heart rate, and body temperature to measure human emotion. Its aim is to bridge the gap between human emotions and computational technology. Emotion is basic in human experience as it influences cognition, perception, learning, communication, and decision-making. It is an interdisciplinary field spanning computer science, engineering, psychology, cognitive science, neuroscience, sociology, education, psychophysiology, ethics, etc.

An affective computing technology senses the emotional state of a user (via sensors, cameras, etc.) and responds by performing a specific feature. It uses various methods including keyboard keystroke, mouse movements analyzing, touch screen interactions processing, facial expression recognition, voice recognition, natural language processing, gestures and body movement recognition, EEG signal processing, etc. [5]. For example, researchers have been exploring the possibility of the voice to carry signals of emotion.

Scientists all over the world have joined forces with engineers, neurologists and psychologists to find measurable indicators of human emotion. Researchers are creating computer algorithms to differentiate levels of pain and developing a range of emotion-sensing devices spanning areas from pain to depression. Their ultimate goal is to develop a low-cost wearable system that could be embedded in trousers, in shoes or a jacket to monitor pain levels.

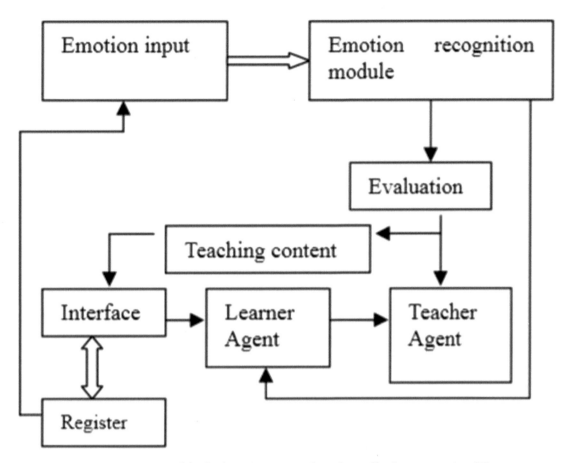

Figure 16.2 A model of e-learning system based on affective computing [7].

16.3 APPLICATIONS

The primary aim of affective computing applications is to build computing systems and devices that express emotions. Common applications of AC include e-therapy (online delivery of psychological health services), Internet-based therapy, special education, neuroscience and autism, customer relationship management, human resource management, marketing, social robots, and computer games (entertainments). Applications for affective computing in all aspects of life are endless. We will consider the following typical applications

- *Special Education:* Computers are currently used for instruction and assisting special education students. Affective computing can benefit the field of special education [6]. E-learning as a learning system has become popular in recent years. As a remote learning, e-learning lacks the emotional communication between computerized tutor and the learner. E-learning programs could automatically detect when the learner was having difficulty and provide additional explanations.

A model of e-learning system based on affective computing is shown in Figure 16.2 [7]. Affective computing can be used to adjust the presentation style of the tutor when a learner is bored or displeased.

- *Gaming:* This is a novel application that combines ideas from affective computing and gaming, which has become a mainstream form of entertainment. Affective gaming has received much attention in the gaming community as they recognize the importance of emotion in the development of engaging games. Video games are invading our daily life and generating substantial revenues for the gaming industry. Affective video games can access their players' emotional states through biofeedback devices. The game detects user's level of stress and uses it to influence the affective state. Affective gaming focuses on sensing and recognizing player's emotions, as well as reducing frustration and inducing pleasurable game challenge[8-10].

- *Human-Computer Interaction:* Affective computing is essentially human-computer interaction (HCI) in which a device has the ability to detect and respond to its user's emotions. The recent developments in HCI have emphasized user-centered rather than computer-centered approach. This led to design of intelligent and affective interfaces. Important discoveries in neuroscience and psychology have contributed to an interest in the scientific study of emotion [11]. Without the ability to process such affect or emotion information, computers cannot be expected to communicate with humans in a natural way. Computers can be trained and programmed to scan a conversation between people and determine whether the participants are angry or happy. Graphical user interface (GUI) is becoming more intelligent for human interests.

- *Healthcare:* Affective computing is also being used in developing communicative technologies for use by people with autism. It can help physicians understand a remote patient's mood or signs of depression. AC technology can sense when one is distracted and can contact emergency services in case of emergency.

- *Surveillance*: The main justification for public surveillance networks is that they are a deterrent to crime. Surveillance technologies have become part of this era of ubiquitous computing with thousands of cameras installed on lampposts and at intersections in cities. The weakest links in surveillance systems are the people monitoring the cameras who may get bored with time. Building an AC system for the purpose of surveillance will eliminate the problem [12].

16.4 BENEFITS

The importance and usefulness of affective computing is reflected by its wide applications in different areas as mentioned in the previous section. Affective computing has the potential to humanize digital interactions and offer benefits in a wide range of applications. AC technology can play an important role in the next generation of biometric surveillance systems. Affective computing features will constitute a defining feature of Web 3.0. Wearable computers are the first application field, having direct access to their users. Affective computing, coupled with wearable computers, will provide the ability to gather new data necessary for advances in emotion, emotional intelligence, and cognition theory.

16.5 CHALLENGES

Affective computing is still in its infancy, and many of the issues and challenges are yet to be resolved. These challenges make AC an open research area. One of the challenges in building emotionally intelligent devices is the automatic recognition of affective states.

AC requires the emotion to be measured quantitatively. Some question the extent to which affective sensing can support the kinds of applications proposed in the literature.

Like humans, emotionally capable computers have the ability to mislead and deceive users. Building simulated affects into artifacts creates a moral dilemma. The so-called "emotional" machines are not really emotional. There is fundamental deception involved in assuming that the machines actually have affective states [13].

When little progress has been made with cognitive modeling, how can one expect much progress in modeling the more subtle and multimodal processes that characterize emotional responses. To the extent that computers do not have physical bodies, they cannot reliably express emotion [14].

To achieve a high accuracy in emotion recognition measurement with reliable precision is difficult. A challenge to a multimodel-based affective recognition system is how to integrate the multimodel information. It is hard to develop a multimodel's affective database because emotion signals are presented in different data types or formats [15].

Existing models in affective computing often use highly stereotyped personality types and emotional responses, which do not relate well to actual behavior. Developing an affective computing design that cannot interact with real human behavior is not desirable [16].

Privacy is a major challenge not only in mobile AC but in the broader area of smart phone sensing. This concern grows dramatically when health or affective data are collected. There are privacy concerns with wearing a camera that records those around you. However, not all kinds of mobile data pose potential threats [17].

Another issue is generalization. Generalization is the capacity to apply knowledge from one context to another. Computers have problems generalizing from the examples they were trained on, to the analysis of new unseen information. The field of machine learning is perpetually trying to improve the ability of computers to generalize [18].

There are a number of other issues addressed in the literature. Physiological readings tend to be inconsistent and contradictory. There are large differences between individuals in their degree of physiological response. We still know very little about the workings of the brain and the realization of affective phenomena within the human body and brain.

Creative exploration of these issues may lead to more fruitful applications of affective computing [19]. More research is needed to improve our understanding of the cognitive representation of emotions.

16.6 CONCLUSION

Recognition of human emotions is a step into the future of artificial intelligence to have computing devices behave like humans. Affective computing is a cross-disciplinary field involving researchers working in various areas ranging from psychiatry to engineering.

Its aim is to build computer systems that express emotions or engineering systems that integrate human affections. It is still in its infancy, and many of the issues and challenges are yet to be resolved.

These challenges make AC an open research area. AC research aims to consider human emotions in the design of new computing systems and devices.

Although affective computing is not a new field, it is becoming more and more relevant today. The age of the emotional machines is fast approaching. Affective computing is posed to revolutionize the way retailers, healthcare givers, governments, and academia sense, gather, organize, and convey information using computers. A number of institutions are sponsoring AC development. The MIT Media Lab hosts the Affective Computing Group. More information on affective computing can be found in the books in [1, 20-27] and in the journal exclusively devoted to it: *IEEE Transactions on Affective Computing.*

REFERENCES

[1]   R. W. Picard, *Affective Computing.* Cambridge, MA: MIT Press, 1997.

[2]   R. W. Picard, "Affective computing: From laughter to IEEE," *IEEE Transactions on Affective Computing,* vol. 1, no. 1, June 2010, pp. 11-17.

[3]   M. N. O. Sadiku, A. E. Shadare, and S. M. Musa, "Affective computing," *International Journal of Trend in Research and Development,* vol. 5, no. 6, Nov.-Dec. 2018, pp. 144-145.

[4]   K. Bakhtiyari, M. Taghavi, and Hafizah Husain, "Hybrid affective computing—Keyboard, mouse and touch screen: From review to experiment," *Neural Computing & Applications,* vol.26, 2015, pp. 1277–1296.

[5]   K. Bakhtiyari and H. Husain, "Fuzzy model of dominance emotions in affective computing," *Neural Computing and Applications,* vol. 25, no. 6, Nov. 2014, pp. 1467–1477.

[6]   M. M. Steele and J. W. Steele, "Applying affective computing techniques to the field of special education," *Journal of Research on Computing in Education,* vol. 35, no. 2, 2002, pp. 236-240.

[7]   S. Duo and L. X. Song, "An e-learning system based on affective computing," *Physics Procedia,* vol. 24, 2012, pp. 1893 – 1898.

[8]   "Affective computing," *Wikipedia,* the free encyclopedia https://en.wikipedia.org/wiki/Affective_computing

[9]   L. Chittaron and R. Sionin, "Affective computing vs. affective placebo: Study of a biofeedback-controlled game for relaxation training," *International Journal of Human-Computer Studies,* vol. 72, 2014, pp. 663-673.

[10] Y.Y. Ng, C.W. Khong, and H. Thwaites, "A review of affective design towards video games," *Procedia - Social and Behavioral Sciences,* vol. 51, 2012, pp. 687 – 691.

[11] R. W. Picard, "Affective computing for HCI," *Proceedings of HCI International (the 8th International Conference on Human-Computer Interaction) on Human-Computer Interaction: Ergonomics and User Interfaces,* August 1999, pp. 829-833.

[12] J. Bullington, "'Affective' computing and emotion recognition systems: The future of biometric surveillance?" *Proceedings of the 2nd annual conference on Information security curriculum development,* 2005, pp. 95-99.

[13] R. D. Warda and P.H. Marsden, "Affective computing: Problems, reactions and intentions," *Interacting with Computers,* vol.16, 2004, pp. 707–713.

[14] R. W. Picard, "Affective computing: Challenges," *International Journal on Human-Computer Studies,* vol. 59, 2003, pp. 55–64.

[15] C. H. Wu, Y. M. Huang, and J. P. Hwang, "Review of affective computing in education/learning: Trends and challenges," *British Journal of Educational Technology*, vol. 47, no. 6, 2016, pp. 1304–1323.

[16] J. D. Schwark, "Toward a taxonomy of affective computing," *International Journal of Human–Computer Interaction*, vol. 31, 2015, pp. 761–768.

[17] E. Politou, E, Alepis, and C. Patsakis, "A survey on mobile affective computing," *Computer Science Review*, 2017, in press, http://dx.doi.org/10.1016/j.cosrev.2017.07.002.

[18] R. Kaliouby, R. Picard, and S. B. Cohen, "Affective computing and autism," *Annals of New York Academy of Sciences*, vol. 1093, 2006, pp. 228–248.

[19] R.D. Ward and P. H. Marsden, "Affective computing: problems, reactions and intentions," *Interacting with Computers*, vol. 16, 2004, pp. 707–713.

[20] R. A. Calvo et al., *The Oxford Handbook of Affective Computing*. Oxford University Press, 2015.

[21] K. R. Scherer, T. Banziger, and E. B. Roesch, *Blueprint for Affective Computing: A Sourcebook*. Oxford University Press, 2010.

[22] J. Tao, T. Tan, and R. W. Picard (eds.), *Affective Computing and Intelligent Interaction*. Berlin, Germany: Springer-Verlag, 2005.

[23] M. J. Wooldridge and M. Veloso (eds.), *Artificial Intelligence Today: Recent Trends and Development*. Springer, 1999.

[24] K. Ahmad (ed.), *Affective Computing and Sentiment Analysis: Emotion, Metaphor and Terminology*. Springer, 2011.

[25] J. Luo, *Affective Computing and Intelligent Interaction*. Springer, 2012.

[26] J. Or (ed.), *Affective Computing*. I-Tech Education and Publishing, 2008.

[27] A. Hussain and E. Cambria, *Socio-Affective Computing*. Springer, 2016.

17

LOCATION-AWARE COMPUTING

Cowards die many times before their death, the valiant never taste of death but once.
- William Shakespeare

17.1 INTRODUCTION

We all have experienced the revolutionary applications that the global positioning system (GPS) and outdoor location services have provided. The advances in mobile computing, location sensing, mobile computing, and wireless networking are giving rise to opportunities in the domain of location-aware or location-based computing. They have led to a new class of computing, namely location-aware computing. Location-awareness concerns the use of information about a person's geographical location to provide more relevant information and services to that person. Location-aware systems play a central role in ubiquitous computing to sense and react to real-world context. There is no longer any excuse for getting lost.

Location-aware computing (LAC) (or location-based computing) refers to computing that takes into account a particular context (mainly position). Location-aware technology is any technology that is able to detect its current location and then manipulate this data to control events. It is a technology that uses the location of people and devices to derive contextual information. Objects which move, such as people and devices, are electronically tagged. LAC coupled with other technologies can transform the world, as illustrated in Figure 17.1 [1].

The aim of this chapter is to provide an introduction to location-aware computing. It begins by covering the basics of location-aware computing and its enabling technologies. It then presents its applications, benefits, and challenges. The last section concludes with some comments.

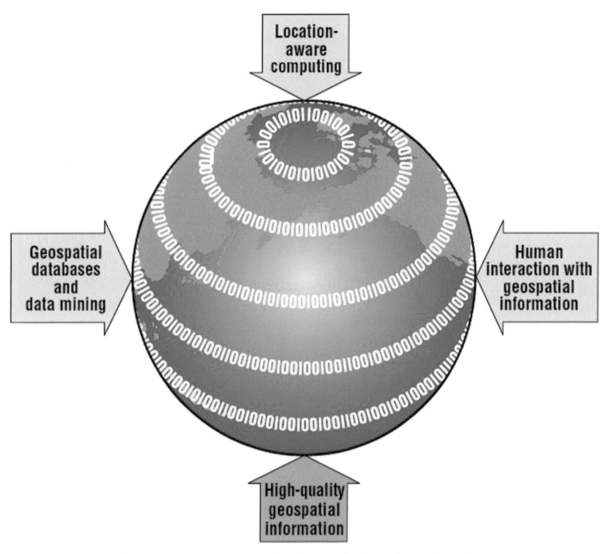

Figure 17.1 Location-aware technology with three other independent technological advances can transform the world [1].

17.2 LOCATION-AWARENESS COMPUTING BASICS

Location-aware computing relies on location-based services, which are tied to mobile networks. It uses location information to improve the value of a wireless network for the users. It may also be regarded as distributed computing activities which are meant to acquire, manage, store, and retrieve the real-time geographical location of mobile users and provides intelligent services. Locating the user terminal, often known as positioning, is essential to location-aware computing. Positioning systems vary widely in their accuracy and precision characteristics. A device's location is usually determined by GPS satellite tracking, cellular tower triangulation, global system for mobile communications (GSM) or wireless fidelity (Wi-Fi).

Location awareness refers to some means of tracking, be it GPS, radio bearing, or conventional ultrasonic, or infrared tracking systems. Location-aware computing system often responds to a user's location, either spontaneously or when activated by a user request. The components of a location-aware system are shown in Figure 17.2 [2]. The system is designed for three types of users [3]: customers, retailers, and database administrators. Using the system, a customer can track sale information at any particular locations using a mobile device. A retailer can update merchandise-related information for their store. The database manager can update location related information.

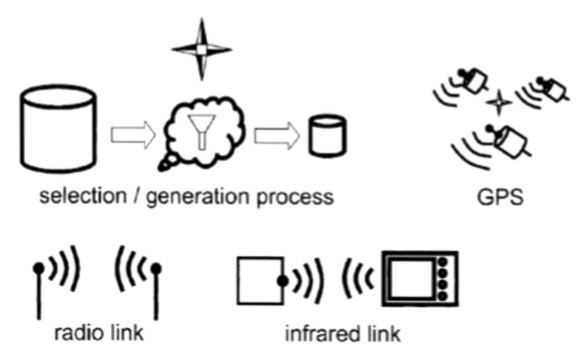

Figure 17.2 Components of a location aware system [2].

17.3 ENABLING TECHNOLOGIES

One of the key enabling technologies for location-aware computing is positioning systems which vary widely in their accuracy and precision. It makes it possible for a receiver to deduce its latitude, longitude, and altitude with an accuracy of a few meters.

Location-aware computing is made possible by three distinct technical capabilities: location and orientation sensing, wireless communication, and mobile computing systems [4].

- *Location and orientation sensing:* A central problem in location-aware computing is the determination of physical location of individuals and devices. Sensor networks enable devices to become interconnected with one another and with the Internet. Sensor technology, such as RFID, could enable mobile devices to extract information from user position automatically. Figure 17.3 shows the location-sensing technologies [5]. These technologies raise many exciting possibilities for the communication and delivery of services among users, devices, and places. Triangulation uses the geometric properties of triangles to compute object locations. Today, the global positioning system (GPS) is the most popular location-sensing system for applications in open, outdoor areas, because it is available to users anywhere on the world and provide three dimensions of information without any network support. Unfortunately, GPS does not work indoors and its error can be intolerable for some applications.

- *Wireless communication:* The IEEE 802.11 family of wireless LAN technologies (IEEE, 1997) is now widely embraced. Wi-Fi is deployed almost everywhere and widely supported on commercial smartphones. Most Wi–Fi networks are protected and do not allow anonymous users to connect to them. Infrared wireless communication is the lowest-cost wireless technology available today. Bluetooth is a wireless protocol that is used for low-power consumption and short range communication (1-100 meters). It is designed primarily for connecting devices such as mobile phones, printers, laptops, and digital cameras. Simple cell-based radio networks include WLAN and GSM. GSM can function both indoor and outdoor.

• *Mobile computing systems:* As the world is becoming increasingly mobile, mobile devices such as smartphones and tablets are replacing desktops to become the main personal computing platforms. Mobile devices allow individuals traveling between places to have real-time access to an increasing variety of information. Laptops and handheld computers are now extensively used for mobile computing. Mobile computing platforms allow users to make use of the mobile data access that wireless communications provide and take advantage of the location context of data. Mobile wireless communication hides the location of mobile equipment from applications and ensuring a consistent quality of service. Mobility is inherently vulnerable and the vulnerability of mobile systems extends to the privacy and confidentiality of the data.

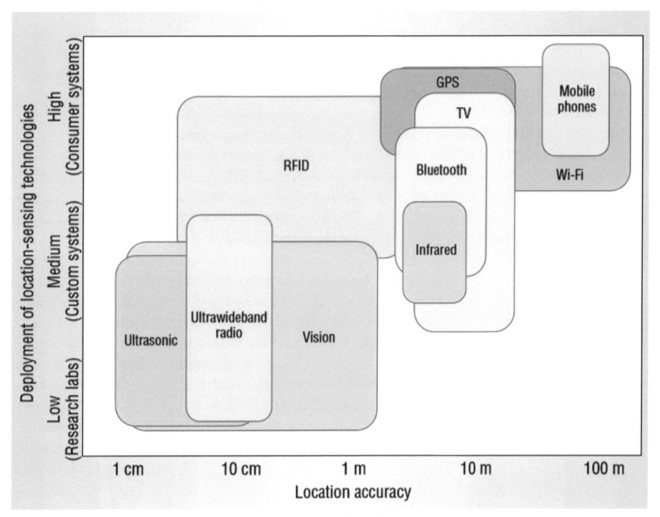

Figure 17.3. Location-sensing technologies [5].

17.4 APPLICATIONS

Location-aware systems focuses on the acquisition of coordinates in a grid. Location-aware technology is increasingly being used in location guidance, especially in GPS navigation of vehicles and for directing tourists in big cities. It can be used to guide new students to specific locations such as classrooms and laboratories on a large campus.

It can be used to indicate wave conditions for commercial fishermen, notify traffic congestion, or warn about severe weather conditions. These applications use predefined content based on location and most of them are still at the stage of research prototypes [6]. Other current applications include camera memory cards, apps on smartphones, supply chain management, healthcare device management, construction industry, friend and family tracking in cellular networks, multi-player online gaming support, security sensitive area protection in cities, and indoor environments, and collision avoidance for air traffic control. Location-aware system can be integrated in ubiquitous computing infrastructure.

17.5 BENEFITS AND CHALLENGES

Location awareness is an important ingredient to many applications of mobile devices. Devices which have the ability to determine their own position in space can retrieve, filter, or present information appropriate to this position [7]. Location-aware computing can improve several aspects of wireless network performance and usability [8]. More and more service providers are developing and deploying location-aware services for consumers.

There are some challenges that will have to be addressed before location-aware computing can become mainstream. The real world constraints limit the efficiency of location aware technologies. As location-aware computing technologies become more prevalent, location privacy concerns are increasingly becoming important. Privacy is considered as a fundamental human right. The central issue in location privacy is the control of location information. How users attempt to manage complex privacy issues has implications for the privacy and security of persons, places, and systems [9]. Some users are not comfortable about their movements being tracked, and are therefore unwilling to use devices revealing their location. Access control must be imposed on location information to prevent unauthorized distribution. This is necessary to retain users' privacy and prevent abuse. The government can act as a catalyst by funding the creation and maintenance of large-scale experimental infrastructure for validating concepts.

The adoption of location-aware computing will be hindered as long as the costs of deploying and managing location-sensing systems remain high. Another challenge is development in viable infrastructure for location-sensing. There are no standards because the market is not large, and big IT leaders have not fully participated. Location-aware computing systems must be designed to cope with these challenges. Credible solutions to the problems are necessary for location-service providers to be commercially viable.

17.6 CONCLUSION

Location-aware computing refers to the ability to provide users with services that depend on their position. It is a new field of research that allows the users to take full advantage of terminal mobility and the location context of data. Locating the user terminal, often called positioning, is essential in location-aware computing. In order to be widely adopted, location-aware computing must be as effortless, familiar, and rewarding as web search tools like Google [10].

REFERENCES

[1] C. A. Patterson, R. R. Muntz, and C. M. Pancake, "Challenges in location aware computing," *Pervasive Computing,* April-June 2003, pp. 80-89.

[2] A. Butz, "Between location awareness and aware locations: Where to put the intelligence," *Applied Artificial Intelligence*, vol. 18, no. 6, 2004, pp.501-512.

[3] C. Wang, "Location-aware consumer information system," *Master's Thesis,* The University of New Brunswick, December, 2007.

[4] "Location-aware computing." National Research Council. 2003. *IT Roadmap to a Geospatial Future.* Washington, DC: The National Academies Press, 2003.

[5] M. Hazas, J. Scott, and J. Krumm, "Location-aware computing comes of age," *Computer,* February 2004, pp. 95-97.

[6] M. N. O. Sadiku, Y. Wang, S. Cui, S. M. Musa, "Location Aware Computing," *International Journal of Advanced Research in Computer Science and Software Engineering*, vol. 9, No. 5, pp. 75-77, May 2019.

[7] A. Butz, "Between location awareness and aware locations: Where to put the intelligence," *Applied Artificial Intelligence*, vol. 18, no. 6, 2004, pp. 501-512.

[8] M. McGuire, E. Hyun, and M. Sima, "Location aware computing for academic environments," *Proceedings of Mobile Content Quality of Experience,* August 2007.

[9] D. Anthony, D. Kotz, and T. Henderson, "Privacy in location-aware computing Environments," *Pervasive Computing,* October-December 2007, pp. 64-72.

[10] B. N. Schilit et al, "Challenge: Ubiquitous location-aware computing and the 'Place Lab' initiative," *Proceedings of the 1st ACM international workshop on Wireless mobile applications and services on WLAN hotspots*, San Diego, CA, September 2003.4

18
CHAPTER

CONTEXT-AWARE COMPUTING

Successful people make decisions quickly as soon as all the facts are available and change them very slowly if ever. Unsuccessful people made decisions very slowly, and change them often and quickly.
- Napoleon Hill

18.1 INTRODUCTION

Today smart phones are seen everywhere since work and social mobility is on the increase. Their success is the reason for shifting towards developing context-aware mobile applications that proactively react to user's environment [1]. Smart phones can detect and react on contextual data due to their multiple sensors and processing capability. Such behaviour is known as context-aware.

Context-aware computing (also known as context sensitive computing) is having computing devices understand the real world and automatically provide appropriate services. To use "context" effectively, we must understand what it is and how it is used.

"Context" is any information that can be used to characterize the situation of an entity, which may be a person, place, or object. It refers to a representation of the environment or surrounding where the system operates. Examples of context are shown in Figure 18.1 [2]. Some context such as time and location may act as sources of contextual information for deriving other contexts [3]. Context-aware is used more generally to include nearby people, devices, lighting, noise level, and network availability. Temperature, humidity, light sensors, and accelerometer can be used to capture some of the aspects of the contexts. Context may be changing rapidly such as in handheld and ubiquitous computing. Figure 18.2 shows a typical workflow of context-aware entities [4].

This chapter provides an introduction to context-aware computing and context-aware systems. It begins by explaining the concept of context-awareness. Then it explains context-aware systems (CAS) and context-aware computing (CAC). It presents their applications, benefits, and challenges. The last section concludes with some comments.

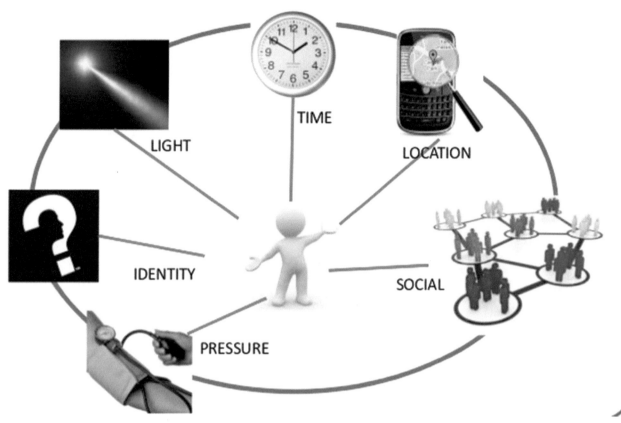

Figure 18.1 Examples of context [2].

18.2 CONCEPT OF CONTEXT-AWARENESS

Our daily living experiences can be simplified by computing systems that are aware of an individual's context. By context, we mean any information which can be used to characterize the situation of an entity, which may be a person, device, place, or object.

Contextual information falls into a wide range of categories including time, location, device, identity, user, role, activity, task, process, and nearby devices/users. Context may refer to [5]: (1) Computing/communication context (network connectivity, resource accessibility), (2) User context (user profile, location, activity), (3) Physical context (temperature, noise level, traffic conditions), (4) Time context (hour, day, week, season, year). Context awareness can by employed at two levels: low/hardware level and high/software level. At the hardware level, context-awareness is employed to facilitate tasks such as routing, modeling, and storage. The software level has access to a wide range of data, knowledge and sources. These enable complex reasoning to be performed [6]. Context may be derived by aggregating data from sensors. Due to advances in sensor technology, sensors are getting more powerful, cheaper, smaller in size, and deployed in a large number.

The term "context-aware" was first introduced by Schilit and Theimer in 1994. Since then, there has been a growing community of researchers orbiting around it. Context- awareness captures the idea that technology plays a more proactive role in our lives. It is a user-centric view of computing and it leads to automation, adaption, and personalization [7]. It is a paradigm in which applications employ contextual information such as time, places, media, people, and activity, etc. as illustrated in Figure 18.3 [8].

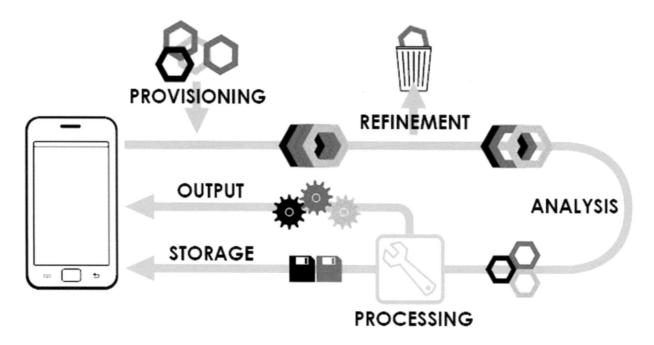

Figure 18.2 A typical workflow of context-aware entities [4].

18.3 CONTEXT-AWARE SYSTEMS

A context-aware system is the system that is aware of its situation/context and can autonomously adapt. It is one that can detect relevant information and adapt in order to improve an interaction. Context-awareness is an important component of most ubiquitous computing applications. It is getting a lot of attention these days since it allows automatic adaptation of devices, systems, and applications to user's context change. The context provides information about the current status of people, places, things, and devices in the environment [9]. Context can be acquired from sensors, middleware infrastructure or context server. It may include an individual's location, blood pressure, or current activities.

Context-aware (or sentient) systems (CASs) are very useful in areas like intelligent environments, pervasive/ ubiquitous computing, fast mobile computing, and ambient intelligence. The systems developed in these emerging fields need to recognize the context in which they are operating. CASs are part of ubiquitous or pervasive computing environment; they sense the users' physical and virtual surrounding to adapt systems behavior accordingly. They offer smart service discovery, delivery and adaptation all based on the current context [10].

A context-aware system (CAS) is an application that adapts to several situations involving user, network, and the application itself. It is one in which applications have knowledge of their surrounding environment, which is composed of people, computing devices, and things. The fundamentals of CAS include context-aware models, context-aware control, context-aware algorithms, context-aware networks, and context-aware computing [11]. The basic components of a typical CAS interacting with a user is shown in Figure 18.4 [12]. Context aware and big data systems are related. Both systems have sensors generating large amounts of data, require big storage spaces, and implement data analytics to infer knowledge from the data.

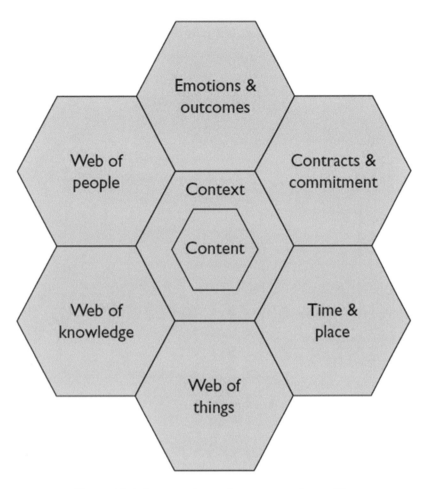

Figure 18.3 Context shapes human experience [8].

18.4 CONTEXT-AWARE COMPUTING BASICS

Context-awareness has also been an integral component of computing. Advances in wireless networking, sensor technologies, and miniaturization, are making computers to be available everywhere and to have a greater awareness of the dynamic environment they are a part of. Computation is now packaged in a variety of devices we use every day.

Context-aware computing is a mobile computing paradigm where applications and services take advantage of contextual information, which may come from multiple sources such as sensors, wearable and portable computers, etc. It is emerging as an effective paradigm for enabling the development of smart services. It refers to a mobile systems that can sense their physical environment and adapt their behavior accordingly.

The concept of context-aware computing (CAC) originated from ubiquitous computing, where the center of computing shifts from machine to human. Ubiquitous computing encompasses a wide spectrum of devices such as smartphones, cameras, games consoles, automatic teller machines, vehicle control systems, household appliances, and computer peripherals such as routers and printers [13, 14]. The goal of CAC is to use context as an implicit cue to enrich the interaction from humans to computers, making it easier to interact with computers. CAC promises to provide a better future in daily computation.

Context-aware computing has the following characteristics [15]:

- *Sentience/Sensing:* This is the ability to perceive change in the user's environment
- *Autonomy:* This is the ability to respond without the user's intervention
- *Adaptation:* This is the ability to offer different behaviors to suit user's needs

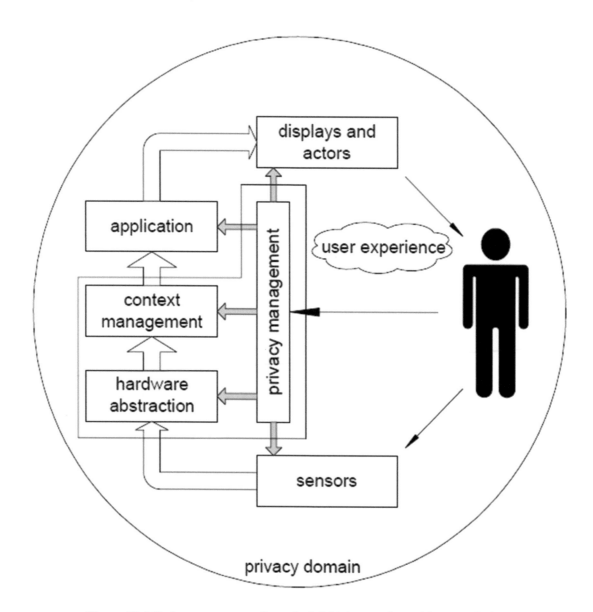

Figure 18.4 Basic components of a typical CAS interacting with a user [12].

18.5 APPLICATIONS

Context-aware systems can be implemented in several ways depending on requirements and conditions such as location of sensors. Different kinds of services and applications of CAC can be seen everywhere such as information communication technology (ICT), health science, humanity, social science, etc. Context-aware applications can adapt their behaviour according to the context and act autonomously. They are widely used with mobile devices.

Context-awareness is the key enabler for ubiquitous computing. Some regard this level of integration of computing technologies as the ultimate goal for computers. Computers have already pervaded our lives, phones, fridges, TVs, alarm clocks, etc. but they will be more useful if they have capability r to be aware of their surroundings, i.e. context-awareness [16].

The first context-aware systems were active badges, which recognize the user's whereabouts. Next was making mobile phones to be context-aware by using MEMS sensors [17]. Efforts were made to integrate intelligence into everyday objects such as headphones, mobile assistants, coffee cups, and furniture.

In the Internet of things environment, things will sense more data and become context-aware. Context-aware information may offer substantial value to manufacturing. Context-awareness can be used in a manufacturing environment to increase the visibility and performance of operations [18].

Over the years, engineers and researchers have developed some prototypes using context-aware computing techniques. Context-aware Systems (CASs) can be found in the areas of wearable computing, mobile computing, robotics, manufacturing, monitoring system, and intelligent user interfaces. Other applications include [19]: (1) customer communications, (2) mobile marketing, (3) connected billboards, (4) smart digital signage, (5) hassle-free access, (6) in-store shopping experience, (7) airport experience, (8) employee training, (9) healthcare, (10) mobile learning system, (11) industrial assembly, (12) intelligent transportation, (13) automatic biometric recognition system, and (14) information security. Major industry leaders like Coca-Cola, Citi, IBM, and Zurich Insurance are just a sampling of those investing in context-aware technology.

18.6 BENEFITS

The major advantage of context-awareness is that it allows for the design of applications that can use information about context to automatically adapt their behavior to a dynamic environment [20]. For example, it is not feasible to process all the data collected by sensors connected to the Internet of things. Context-awareness becomes important in deciding what need should be processed [21].

Potential beneficiaries of context-aware computing and systems range from homes to workplaces and from civil domains to military domains. Context-awareness has been applied to the area of computer-supported cooperative work to help employees work and collaborate more efficiently with each other. Several researchers have developed context-aware services to demonstrate the usefulness of the new technology.

The context-aware computing is regarded as a key enabling technology in realizing ubiquitous or pervasive computing systems, which seek to deal with linking changes in the environment with computer systems.

18.7 CHALLENGES

A context-aware computing system is generally distributed, large scale, and complex. Because of its complexity, it is difficult to develop such a system. Context-aware computing has not found commercial success yet. It has not been possible to apply context-awareness in practical systems. Managing context in IoT is fraught with challenges. CAC has proven to be successful in understanding sensor data.

Context awareness is one of the major challenges to be addressed when developing ubiquitous computing systems. To implement a CAS requires addressing some issues [22]: How does the system represent context internally? How frequently does the system need to consult contextual information? It has been argued that there are human aspects of context that cannot be sensed by technological means, not to talk about CAS acting on our behalf. Because of this, the commercial application of CAS is still restricted to sensing [23].

Besides this, many issues remain to be addressed. Security and privacy issues often do not receive enough attention. Another major issue is trust, which is somewhat determined by system reliability. We cannot often assume systems are highly reliable because context information is often incomplete and imperfect [24]. In mobile CAS, the incompleteness of information is in terms of missing data, while the imperfectness indicate uncertain context. These issues should be taken into consideration from the initial stages of the design.

18.8 CONCLUSION

Context awareness refers to the perception of the environment and the ability to act accordingly. A context-aware system is a ubiquitous system, which is able to adapt its behavior automatically according to the gathered context information. The context-aware nature is regarded as a key factor in realizing ubiquitous computing systems. Two main technologies that make ubiquitous computing feasible are portable computers and wireless communications. Context-aware applications employ context information to guide their behaviour. Context-aware computing provides situation-specific services. It is an important component of a pervasive computing or ubiquitous computing (which are used interchangeably) environment. Mobile CAC is an essential aspect of the smart cities infrastructure.

CAC is a disruptive technology that is capable of transforming and enriching human experience. It is poised to drastically change how we interact with our devices. Future devices will learn about you, the restaurants you have picked in the past, how you liked the food, and then make suggestions for restaurants nearby based on experience. Context aware systems are a promising approach to facilitate and mediate communication in our daily-life activities. They are a potential technology for mobile devices. They are going to shape computing and communication of the future. More information about context-aware computing and systems can be found in the books in [25-29].

REFERENCES

[1]   C. Dobre, "CAPIM: A platform for context-aware computing," *Proceedings of International Conference on P2P, Parallel, Grid, Cloud and Internet Computingr.* 2014, pp. 266-272.

[2]   S. A. Sonawane, Context-aware computing," https://www.slideshare.net/swatibaiger/context-aware-computing-14084995

[3]   S. Poslad, "Context-aware systems," in *Ubiquitous Computing: Smart Devices, Environment and Interactions.* Chichester, UK: John Wiley & Sons, 2009, chapter 7, pp. 214-244.

[4]   C. Schmidt, "Context-aware computing," https://www.snet.tu-berlin.de/fileadmin/fg220/courses/WS1011/snet-project/context-aware-computing_schmidt.pdf

[5]   K. P. Subbu and A. V. Vasilakos, "Big data for context aware computing – Perspectives and challenges," *Big Data Research*, vol. 10, 2017, pp. 33-43.

[6]   C. Perera et al., "Context aware computing for the Internet of things: a survey," *IEEE Communications Surveys & Tutorials,* vol. 16, no.1, First Quarter, pp. 414-454.

[7] M. N. O. Sadiku, C. M. M. Kotteti, S. M. Musa, "Context-aware omputing," *Journal of Scientific and Engineering Research*, vol. 5, no. 7, 2018, pp. 159-162.

[8] P. Mehra, "Context-aware computing: Beyond search and location-based services," *IEEE Internet Computing*, March/April 2012, pp. 12-18.

[9] Y. Y. Hong, E. H. Suh, and S. J. Kim, "Context-aware systems: A literature review and classification," *Expert Systems with Applications*, vol. 36, 2009, pp. 8509-8522.

[10] M. N. O. Sadiku, K. G. Eze, and S.M. Musa, "Context-aware systems," *International Journal of Trend in Research and Development*, vol. 5, no. 4, 2018, pp. 1-2.

[11] P. C, Vinh (ed.), "EAI endorsed transactions on context-aware systems and applications," http://eudl.eu/issue/casa/4/14

[12] S. Meyer and A. Rakotonirainy, "A survey of research on context-aware homes," *Worshop on Wearable, Invisible, Context-Aware, Ambient, Pervasive and Ubiquitous Computing*, Adelaide, Australia, 2003.

[13] S. Poslad, *Ubiquitous Computing: Smart Devices, Environments and Interactions*. John Wiley & Sons, 2009.

[14] M. N. O. Sadiku, Y. Wang, S. Cui, and S. M. Musa, "Ubiquitous Computing: A Primer," *International Journal of Advances in Scientific Research and Engineering*, vol. 4, no. 2, February 2018, pp. 28-31.

[15] N. Wang, "Client-server software infrastructure for context-aware applications development," *Master's Thesis*, The University of New Brunswick, November 2006.

[16] A. Schmidt, "Context-aware computing," in C. Ghaoui (ed.), *The Encyclopedia of Human-Computer Interaction*. London, UK: Idea Group Reference, 2nd ed., Chapter 14, 2006.

[17] W. Dargie, "Why is context-aware computing less successful?" *ACM Casemans '11*, Beihing, China, September 2011.

[18] K. Alexopoulos et al., "A concept for context-aware computing in manufacturing: The while goods case," *International Journal of Computer Integrated Manufacturing*, vol. 29, no. 8, 2017, pp. 839-849.

[19] "Our context-aware future: An exploration of context-aware technology and its impact on how we do business," Oracle white paper, March 2016, http://www.oracle.com/us/industries/financial-services/our-context-aware-future-wp-2854928.pdf

[20] M. Benerecetti, P. Bouquet, and M. Bonifacio, "Distributed context-aware systems," *Human-Computer Interaction*, vol. 16, no. 2-4, 2011, pp. 213-228.

[21] K. Yang and S. B. Cho, "A context-aware system in Internet of things using modular Bayesian networks," *International Journal of Distributed Sensor Networks*, vol. 13, no. 5, 2017.

[22] M. Satyanarayanan, "Challenges in implementing a context-aware system," *Pervasive Computing*, 2002, p. 2.

[23] V. Belloti and K. Edwards, "Intelligibility and accountability: Human considerations in context-aware systems," *Human-Computer Interaction*, vol. 16, no. 4, 2001, pp. 193-212.

[24] S. Antifakos et al., "Towards improving trust in context-aware systems by displaying system confidence," *Proceedings of the 7th international Conference on Human Computer Interaction with Mobile Devices & Services*, Salzburg, Austria, Sept. 2005, pp. 9-14.

[25] L. Feng, *Context-Aware Computing*. De Gruyter, 2018.

[26] K. Curran (ed.), *Recent Advances in Ambient Intelligence and Context-Aware Computing*. Information Science Reference, 2015.

[27] P. Temdee and R. Prasad, *Context-Aware Communication and Computing: Applications for Smart Environment.* Springer, 2018.

[28] M. J. Gajjar, *Mobile Sensors and Context-Aware Computing.* Morgan Kaufmann, 2017.

[29] D. Raz et al., *Fast and Efficient Context-Aware Services.* John Wiley & Sons, 2006.

19
CHAPTER

POWER-AWARE COMPUTING

A man is not finished when he is defeated.
He is finished when he quits.
- Richard Nixon

19.1 INTRODUCTION

Energy and powered devices are an integral part of our modern society. With the proliferation of portable computing devices, power consumption has become a major concern in many research projects and commercial systems. Also, as we approach the limits of scaling in CMOS technologies, power and heat dissipation issues are increasingly important.

Power consumption is important for both mobile devices and tethered devices (connected to a power supply when in use). It is a critical parameter of contemporary integrated circuits, expecting them to consume as little power as possible. Power consumption has posed a serious challenge to the high-performance computing systems. It has become the limiting factor in keeping up with developing faster, smaller, and high performance computers.

To improve the system's power efficiency, various policies have been suggested that aim at minimizing electricity consumption and cooling by powering parts of the system during periods of low load. One current research initiative, which drew much attention to this area, is the Power Aware Computing and Communications (PAC/C) program sponsored by DARPA. The main goal of PAC/C is to improve power consumption using the awareness of power consumption of individual devices that make up the system. Power-aware computing is to minimize energy requirements for computation.

This chapter provides a brief introduction to power-aware computing. It commences with introducing the basics of power-aware computing. It then presents some applications, benefits, and challenges of power-aware computing. The last section concludes with a comment.

19.2 CONCEPT OF POWER- AWARE COMPUTING

Energy is the ability to do work, while power is the rate of energy consumption. Energy is the product of power and time. Energy and power are becoming critical components in computer systems in general, and portable systems, in particular. Energy consumption or energy efficiency has become the limiting factor in the development of faster, smaller computer systems such as smartphones. People are often more interested in power than energy, as it shows the rate of energy usage [1]. The energy consumption of a device is often measured via a power meter.

The notion of power-aware (or low-power) computing is not new. The main objective of power-aware computing is to conserve energy for routing messages from source to destination. Power-awareness has increasingly become an important issue in high-performance computing (HPC), where performance is defined as speed and power consumption increases with performance. The explosive growth in the number of components in computing systems will cause a dramatic increase in system power requirements.

The goal of power-aware computing (or energy-aware computing) is to minimize energy requirements for computation, by treating energy as a constrained resource like memory or disk. It is to save energy without compromising on performance. Power-aware design techniques attempt to maximize performance under power dissipation and power consumption constraints.

19.3 APPLICATIONS

Power-aware computing for heterogeneous world-wide grid is a new track of research.

Many applications exhibit a compromise between the accuracy of the result that they produce and the power that they require to produce the result. For example, designers of **g**rid computing who are interested in power-aware technologies should take into account power and energy consumption in order to attract volunteer peers and to guarantee the success of their software.

Power consumption is important for mobile devices due to limitation of their battery life. Better management of power yields longer battery life. It is also important in wearable devices, which are the enabling technology for many applications in healthcare, well-being, military, and smart vehicles.

With the increased use of cloud computing, organizations are becoming aware of wasted power consumed by unutilized resources. The backbone of cloud computing is data centers, which consume a significant amount of energy. Data centers can leverage power management solutions to achieve the targeted computing reliability and economic efficiency. The power management strategies for the data centers would help cloud providers to regulate electricity consumption and reduce cloud computing costs [2].

Energy consumption is critical in wireless sensor networks because the nodes are powered by batteries. A smart sensor is a collection of integrated sensors and electronics. These types of sensors are used to form a wireless sensor networks (WSN), which can be used for monitoring systems in the harsh environment [3].

19.4 BENEFITS AND CHALLENGES

In small devices, better power management translates into longer lasting and smaller batteries. Low-power techniques can lead to a reduction in error. High-performance computing has always been performance-oriented and the power consumption increases with performance. Power-aware computing can achieve significant power reduction and energy savings with minimal impact on performance.

Low-power computing is challenging. Power-aware computing is challenging due to the sheer explosion of total hardware/software decisions. Power supplies and microprocessors are generally designed as separate systems. Some challenges facing power supply designers could be eliminated if there is more interaction between microprocessor designers and power supplies [4]. Direct measurements of CPU power consumption present some technical challenges. Modern application software is still oblivious to power consumption.

A major challenge associated with power consumption in computing devices is the heat they generate. Such heat is often a greater problem than the amount of power consumed. Federal agencies have identified power consumption implications for air quality, national security, and climate change [5]. Since temperature is proportional to power density, methods for reducing thermal effects can also reduce power. The tradeoffs among performance, complexity, cost, and power of electronic systems have created exciting challenges and opportunities. By finding a tradeoff between performance and power consumption it would be possible to control the battery life of mobile devices [6].

19.5 CONCLUSION

Power usage and energy consumption have become important in computing communities, in particular for high performance computing and big data centers. Power-aware computing has attracted the interest of researchers and users of computing systems. A lot of research has been done on the power-aware computing, leading to different techniques and approaches for minimizing power consumption. We need an interdisciplinary scientific approach to design hardware, software, and applications of power-aware computing systems. More information on power-aware computing can be found in books in [7-9].

REFERENCES

[1]   H. Hassan and A. S. Moussa, "Power aware computing survey," *International Journal of Computer Applications*, vol. 90, no. 3, March 2014, pp. 21-26.

[2]   A. Vafamehr and M. E. Khodayar, "Energy-aware cloud computing," *The Electricity Journal*, vol. 31, 2018, pp. 40–49.

[3]   A. Salhieh and L. Schwiebert, "Power-aware metrics for wireless sensor networks," *International Journal of Computers and Applications*, vol. 26, no. 2, 2004, pp. 1-7.

[4]   P. S. Shenoy and P. T. Krein, "Power supply aware computing," *Proceedings of the International Conference on Energy Aware Computing,* December 2010.

[5]   P. Ranganathan, "Recipe for efficiency: Principles of power-aware computing," *Communications of the ACM*, vol. 53, no. 4, April 2010, pp. 60-67.

[6]   M. N. O. Sadiku, A. A. Omotoso, and S. M. Musa, "Power Aware Computing," *International Journal of Trend in Scientific Research and Development*, vol. 4, no. 1, November-December 2019, pp.24-25.

[7]   R. Karri and D. Goodman (eds.), *System-level Power Optimization for Wireless Multimedia Communication: Power Aware Computing.* Kluwer Academic Publishing, 2002.

[8]   R. Graybill and R. Melhem (eds.), *Power Aware Computing.* Springer Science, 2002.

[9]   M. Pedram and J. M. Rabaey, *Power Aware Design Methodologies.* New York: Kluwer Academic Publishers, 2002.

20

SELF-AWARE COMPUTING

Man's capacity for justice makes democracy possible, but man's inclination to justice makes democracy necessary.
- Reinhold Niebuhr

20.1 INTRODUCTION

Computing systems are becoming increasingly complex, heterogeneous, dynamic, and decentralized. Since humans can no longer deal with the rising complexity (which may include scale, uncertainty, and heterogeneity) of the systems, these systems should be enabled to autonomically manage themselves. One approach on how to rise to this challenge is to endow computing systems with increased self-awareness, in order to enable autonomous adaptive behavior [1]. Self-aware computing has arisen as a set of techniques for assisting system developers who must deal with conflicting constraints; e.g., achieving high performance at low power consumption.

In order to effectively manage itself, a system needs knowledge about itself and its environment. Self-awareness is concerned about availability, collection, and representation of knowledge about a system, by that system, and the ways that system can update that knowledge. This knowledge helps in reasoning and smart decision making for adaptive behavior [2].

Self-aware computing systems (SACs) are introspective, adaptive, self-healing, goal-oriented, and approximate. These five key properties enable SACs to be efficient, resilient, and easy to program.

Self-awareness is a familiar concept in the fields of psychology and cognitive science.

There are many instantiations of self-* such as self-adaptive, self-optimizing, self-coordinating and self-healing, as shown in Figure 20.1 [3]. Many experiments have shown that self focused attention has important implications for self-regulation and self-evaluation to occur. Self-awareness is a key attribute in both autonomic and organic computing. The need for self-awareness has arisen in a variety of areas of computer science and engineering in recent years. Advanced organisms also engage in meta-self-awareness, which is a higher level of self-awareness, i.e. an awareness that they themselves are self-aware [4]. For example, meta-self-awareness is needed in selecting between different sensors, actors, learning techniques or between multiple adaptation strategies.

This chapter provides an introduction to self-aware computing. It begins by presenting the levels of self-awareness. Then it addresses the concept and applications of self-aware computing. It covers the benefits and drawbacks/challenges of self-awareness approaches. The last section concludes with some comments.

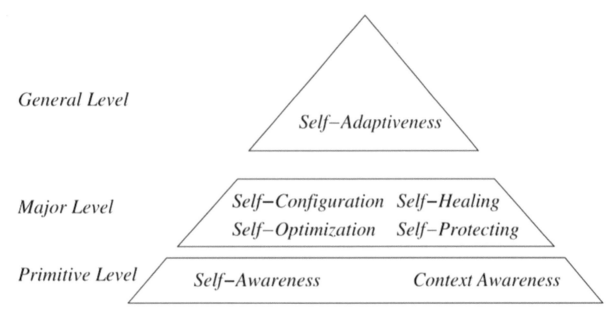

Figure 20. 1. Hierarchy of self-★ properties [3].

20.2 LEVELS OF SELF-AWARENESS

The term self-awareness has been adopted from biology and cognitive science. It refers to the capability of a system to obtain and react upon certain knowledge. It involves developing an understanding of one's emotions and feelings. It is an awareness of the physical, emotional, and psychological self. It is the ability to recognize oneself as an individual separate from other individuals and the environment. It has been proposed as a means for autonomous adaptive behavior for complex systems.

Self-aware computing is a paradigm for structuring and simplifying the design and operation of complex, dynamic computing systems. The self-aware design concept permeates all levels of a computing system such as processor, operating systems, compilers, runtime systems, and applications. There are two types of self-awareness:. private self-awareness and public-awareness. Private self-awareness is agent's internal knowledge only known to agent itself. Public self-awareness is the agent's knowledge about its environment, its role, and social relationship [5].

There are different levels of self-awareness, ranging from basic awareness of environmental stimuli to awareness of one's own thoughts [6, 7]. These are illustrated in Figure 20.2 [2] and explained as follows.

1. *Stimulus-aware:* A node is stimulus-aware if it has knowledge of stimuli. Stimulus-awareness is a prerequisite for all other levels of self-awareness. Since stimuli may originate both internally and externally, stimulus-awareness can either be private, public or both. Private self-awareness refers to a node possessing knowledge of phenomena that are internal to itself. Public self-awareness concerns with a node possessing knowledge of phenomena external to itself.

2. *Interaction-aware:* A node is interaction-aware if it has knowledge that stimuli and its own actions form part of interactions with other nodes and the environment. Through fSedback loops, the

interaction-aware system can learn that its actions can cause specific reactions from its social or physical environments.

3. *Time-aware:* A node is time-aware if it has knowledge or information about history, experience, or likely future phenomena. Implementing time awareness might require having the system use explicit memory.

4. *Goal-aware:* A node is goal-aware if it has knowledge of current goals, objectives, preferences, and constraints. Goal-awareness permits changes in goals, which can be either local or global goals. Self-aware systems work under constraints of user goals.

5. *Meta-self-aware:* A node is meta-self-aware if it has knowledge of its own level(s) of awareness. A meta– self- aware system can adapt the way in which it realizes a self- awareness level.

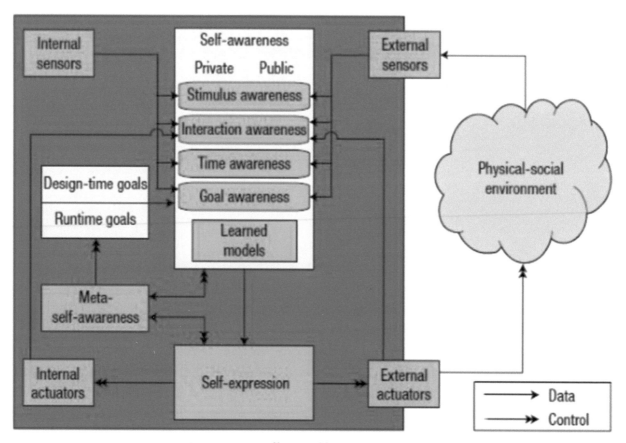

Figure 20.2 Different self-awareness levels [2].

20.3 CONCEPT OF SELF-AWARE COMPUTING

Self-aware computing systems (SACs) are essentially a subclass of autonomic computing systems. They are computing systems that models capturing knowledge about themselves and their environment on an ongoing basis. They are systems that are inspired by self-awareness concepts in humans and animals. They can automatically adjust their behavior and resources to automatically find the best way to meet user specified goals [8]. They can collect information both from internal sensors and external sensors. A comparison between traditional system and self-aware system is made in Figure 20.3 [9]. Traditional, non-adaptive systems, run in an open loop and the application is deployed without the flexibility to change its behavior. In contrast, self-aware systems run in a closed loop so that all layers (hardware, compilers, operating systems, and applications) can observe their environment, alter their decisions, and change their behavior.

A self-aware computer is capable of achieving 10x to 100x improvement in key metrics such as power efficiency and cost performance over extant computers. **S**elf-aware computing is related to autonomic computing and organic computing. In the autonomic computing system, end-users define high-level goals and the system adapts to achieve the desired behavior. The system can alter its behavior to meet multiple goals and automatically adapt to environmental changes. A self-aware system has knowledge and experiences of itself, allowing reasoning and intelligent decision making to support effective, autonomous adaptive behavior. Applications explicitly state goals and the self-aware system continuously monitors itself and adapts its behavior to ensure the goals are met.

The design of self-aware computing systems requires an integrated interdisciplinary approach from multiple areas of computer science and engineering, including software and systems engineering, systems modeling, simulation and analysis, autonomic and organic computing, machine learning and artificial intelligence, data center resource management, etc. How some of these areas are related to self-aware system is illustrated in Figure 20.4 [10].

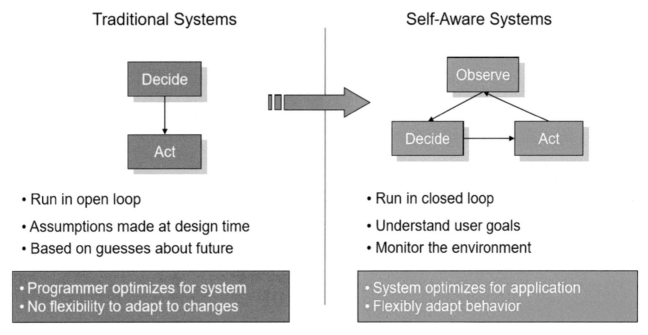

Figure 20.3 Comparison of traditional and self-aware systems [9].

20.4 APPLICATIONS

Self-aware computing systems address a growing need for automation in the management of complex computer applications. They automatically adjust their behavior to help applications achieve their goals. Applications of self-aware computing include autonomic computing, organic computing, control systems, automation, military, enterprise applications, self-awareness of cloud applications, online gaming, robotics, healthcare, and cyber-physical applications [11]. In some of these applications, self-awareness is essential for safety and ethics.

- *DARPA System:* The military is interested in self-aware computing systems that could help soldiers or pilots, for example, on hazardous missions. The systems will automatically study a situation, determine potential actions, and calculate the best alternative. Police officers and firefighters could also benefit from such systems, which are being managed by the US Defense Advanced Research Projects Agency (DARPA) [12].

- *Self-aware Computing Framework* (SEEC): SEEC addresses the problem of automatically and dynamically scheduling actions while balancing competing goals in a fluctuating environment. It automatically and dynamically schedules actions to meet application specified goals. It is designed to incorporate observations made at both the system and application levels [13].

- *Automation:* The IT industry badly needs automation technologies to help deal with some challenges. Automation helps reduce manual labor cost in management and administration. There have been an increasing number of companies that aim at developing automation solutions for capacity planning, provisioning and deployment, service level assurance, anomaly detection, failure/performance diagnosis, high availability, disaster recovery, and security enforcement [14].

- *Robotics:* In autonomous robotics, self-awareness is essential for safety and ethics. Self-awareness is not only a property that is observable at an individual level, but is also something that can arise collectively [15]. In robotics, one is concerned with replicating forms of self-awareness that appear to be human.

- *Cloud Computing*: Cloud applications raise a complex management challenge due to the three main goals of the stakeholders: application users, application operators, and cloud operators. Clouds computing applications are increasingly relying on self-aware management technique [15].

- *Embedded Systems:* These systems need self-awareness to operate autonomously in the face of uncertainty and unpredictability in the environment. They exhibit self-awareness characteristics at various levels. At the heart of such systems are software/hardware computing platforms that interact with the physical world through sensors, actuators, networking, and decision making systems [16].

Developing a SAC application can be noticeably simplified by the support of a middleware system. A middleware system is a software layer located between the operating system and the application. A middleware system can support the application in re-routing data flows [17].

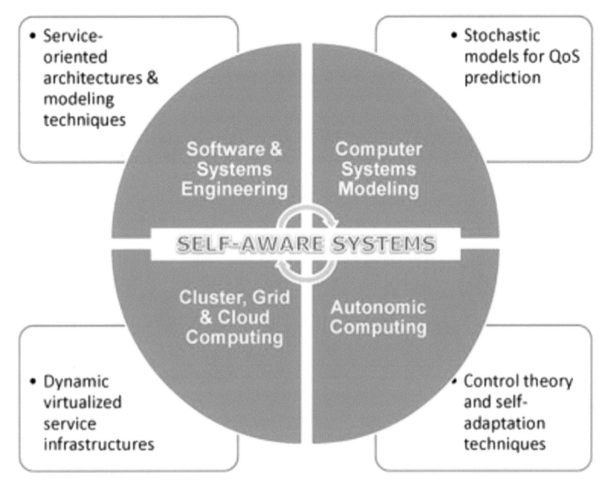

Figure 20.4 How self-aware computing is related to areas of computer science and engineering [10].

20.5 BENEFITS AND CHALLENGES

Awareness is essential because an un-aware computing system can never respond to users and system goals. Self-aware features are used to improve a system's functional value, performance, and robustness. Accurate self-awareness is critical for adapting your behavior to your actual abilities. Individuals become conscious of themselves through the development of self-awareness. They become conscious of their body and mental state including thoughts, actions, ideas, feelings, and interactions with others. Improving self-awareness improves self-control, reduce procrastination, and develop mood management [18]. Self-awareness is crucial for adaptive autonomous systems. It facilitates a proper assessment of cost constrained cyber-physical systems and allocates limited resources where they are most needed. It improves system behavior and reduces processing. Self-aware computing has been used to meet some challenges in modern computing systems.

Self-aware systems have the benefits of increasing self-awareness. But increased self-awareness comes at a cost, whether it be in terms of more processing power or increased storage. It is not feasible to implement self-awareness in an ad hoc manner for a new system.

Due to the huge number of independent, connected devices and the heterogeneity of operating systems, security is of high priority. Privacy and safety are also important in the new evolving environment [19].

20.6 CONCLUSION

Self-awareness is well studied in biology, psychology, medicine, and more recently in engineering and computing. In order to cope with evolving environment and changing user needs, a system should have knowledge about itself and its surroundings. Our concept of computational self-awareness can provide computing systems with autonomous behavior in rapidly changing conditions. Self-aware computing systems are designed to address a growing need for automation in the management of large, complex computer applications. For more information on self-aware computing, one should consult the books in [6, 20, 21].

REFERENCES

[1] M. N. O. Sadiku, M. Tembely, and S.M. Musa, "Self-aware computing: A primer," *International Journal of Advanced Research in Computer Science and Software Engineering*, vol. 9, no. 6, June 2019, pp.39-42.

[2] N. Gill, "Comparison of self-aware and organic computing systems," https://arxiv.org/pdf/1809.10846.pdf

[3] N. Dutt, A. Jantsch, and S. Sarma, "Toward smart embedded systems: A self-aware system-on-chip (SoC) perspective," *ACM Transactions on Embedded Computing Systems*, vol. 15, no. 2, February 2016.

[4] A. Agne et al., "Self-awareness as a model for designing and operating heterogeneous multicores," *ACM Transactions on Reconfigurable Technology and Systems,* vol. 7, no. 2, June 2014.

[5] N. Gill, "Comparison of self-aware and organic computing systems," https://arxiv.org/pdf/1809.10846.pdf

[6] T. Chen et al., *The Handbook of Engineering Self-Aware and Self-Expressive Systems*, 2014, https://arxiv.org/abs/1409.1793

[7] P. R. Lewis, "Architectural aspects of self-aware and self expressive computing systems: From psychology to engineering," *Computer*, vol. 48, no. 8, August 2015, pp. 62-70.

[8] P. R. Lewis, "Self-aware computing systems: From psychology to engineering," *Design, Automation and Test in Europe*, 2017, pp. 1044-1049.

[9] H. Hoffmann et al., "SEEC: A framework for self-aware computing," http://projects.csail.mit.edu/angstrom/SLS/SEEC-120810.pdf

[10] "Vision," http://descartes.ipd.kit.edu/research/vision/index.html

[11] A. Iosup et al., "Self-awareness of cloud applications," In S. Kounev et al. (eds.), *Self-aware Computing Systems*. Springer, 2017., chapter 20, pp. 575-610.

[12] L. D. Paulson, "DARPA creating self-aware computing," *Computer,* vol. 36, no. 3, March 2003, p. 24.

[13] H. Hoffmann et al., "SEEC: A general and extensible framework for self-aware computing," 2011, https://dspace.mit.edu/handle/1721.1/67020

[14] S. Kounev et al. (eds.), "Model-driven algorithms and architectures for self-aware computing systems," January 2015, http://www.dagstuhl.de/15041

[15] P. R. Lewis et al., "Architectural aspects of self-aware and self-expressive computing systems: From psychology to engineering," *Computer*, August 2016, pp. 62-70.

[16] S. Sarma, "Cyber-physical-system-on-chip (CPSoC): An exemplar self-aware SoC and smart computing platform," *Doctoral Dissertation*, University of California, Irvine, 2016.

[17] J. Simonjan, B. Dieber, and B. Rinner, "Middleware support for self-aware computing systems," in P. R. Lewis et al. (eds.), *Self-aware Computing Systems: An Engineering Approach*. Springer, 2016, Chapter 11, pp. 215-238.

[18] "Self-awareness, *Wikipedia,* the free encyclopedia, https://en.wikipedia.org/wiki/Self-awareness

[19] V. Christian, "Pervasive computing: Towards self-aware systems," https://www.pervasive.jku.at/ Research/Publications/_Documents/PervasiveComputingSelfAware-christian2004.pdf

[20] P. R. Lewis et al. (eds.), *Self-aware Computing Systems: An Engineering Approach*. Springer, 2016.

[21] S. Kounev et al. (eds.), *Self-aware Computing Systems*. Springer, 2017.

21

AMORPHOUS COMPUTING

Nothing in the world is difficult for one who sets his mind to do it.
- Chinese saying

21.1 INTRODUCTION

Ideas from computing and biology have been combined to create amorphous computing. The term "amorphous computing" (AC) was coined by a research team at MIT in 1996. They regarded AC as a bio-inspired novel computing paradigm that mimics the way organisms compute [1]. Amorphous computer consists of a large number of tiny interacting computing elements, each with a CPU, memory, and means of communication. An amorphous computing medium is a system of irregularly placed, asynchronous, locally interacting computing elements or agents. Each element is programmed identically and can communicate with a few neighbors.

Amorphous computing refers to computational systems that use very large numbers of identical, parallel processors each having limited computational ability. It draws from biology to help create an entirely new branch of computer science and engineering. The study of amorphous computing aims to identify useful programming methodologies that will enable us to engineer the emergent behavior of a myriad, locally interacting computing elements. The elements or agents run asynchronously, are interconnected in unknown manner, communicate only locally, are identically programmed, and are lacking a rigidly defined architecture for sharing information. Each element has modest computing power and memory. Since the number of particles is assumed to be very large, the entire amorphous medium may be considered as a massively parallel computing system.

Amorphous computations can be naturally found in many fields such as developmental biology, molecular biology, neural networks, and chemical engineering [2]. Recently, amorphous computing has attracted a great interest both as an alternative model of computing and as an inspiration to understand developmental biology. Development in electronics and microfrabrication has made it possible to produce huge number of almost-identical information-processing units at almost no cost.

This chapter provides an introduction on amorphous computing. It begins by addressing the concept of amorphous computing. It covers some applications, benefits, and challenges of amorphous computing. The last section concludes with comments.

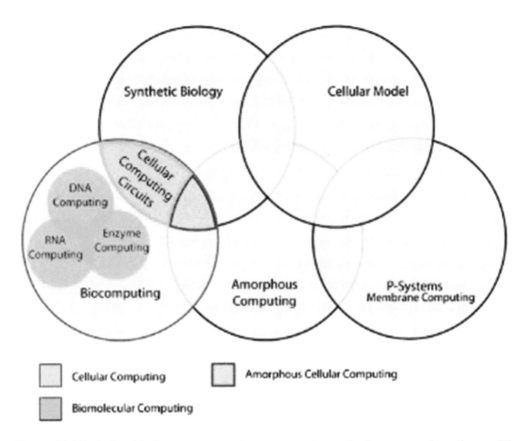

Figure 21.1 Relationship between amorphous computing and other computing schemes [3].

21.2 CONCEPT OF AMORPHOUS COMPUTING

As shown in Figure 21.1, amorphous computing is related to cellular computing, biological computing, and other computing schemes [3]. While cellular computing works well with a multitude of particles cooperating to achieve some computational goal, new aspects of the amorphous computing model are evolvability, asynchrony, and locality. It differs from the traditional computations in many ways. The architecture of amorphous computers is random, whereas there is no room for randomness in classical models such as RAMs [4]. They consist of a set of elements and self-powered processors that can communicate wirelessly over a limited distance. The creation of order in an asynchronous, randomly structured network of cells is the mystery of amorphous computing. The idea of AC is to distribute computations to a large number of locally interacting processing elements rather than implementing sequentially basic instructions.

Amorphous computing is an unconventional computing paradigm that depends on massively parallel execution of computer code by a large number of small, processing units. An amorphous computer consists of several identical processing elements (or agents). Each element has limited computing resources and no global unique identifier [5]. Recent development in nanotechnology will enable inexpensive bulk manufacturing of these tiny processing elements. The elements are physically similar to sand particles and they are referred to as amorphous particles. The particles communicate through broadcast messages, which can only be heard within a radius r of its source. This is illustrated in Figure 21.2 [6]. There is no guarantee that a message will reach its destination due to collisions [7]. A particle may not initially know the distances or directions to any of its neighbors but knows their IDs. The elements do not initially have any information to distinguish themselves from other elements; this includes information about position, identity, and connectivity. Amorphous computing is the study of such computing environment. Swarm intelligence emerges from the collective intelligence of groups of simple autonomous agents.

An amorphous computer consists of a multitude of tiny computers each with a CPU, a modest amount of memory, and communication capability. Each agent can communicate with its neighbors. It is assumed that the number of agents is large and that the entire amorphous medium is a massively parallel computer system. Thus, amorphous computers tend to have the following properties [2]:

- Implemented by redundant, potentially faulty, massively parallel devices.
- Devices having limited memory and computational abilities.
- Devices being asynchronous.
- Devices having no a priori knowledge of their location.
- Devices communicating only locally.
- Exhibit emergent or self-organizational behavior.
- Fault-tolerant, especially to the occasional malformed device.

Any framework with these properties lends itself for amorphous computation. Executing a program on an amorphous computer involves loading the program onto each agent.

An amorphous computing medium consists of independent computational particles, all identically programmed and inspired by nature with computer science techniques for controlling complexity. An amorphous computer system (ACS) consists of a CPU/memory core surrounded by programmable hardware which can be used to enhance the function of the core. Programmable hardware enables the I/O to be tailored to the application during design and fine tuned during system integration and test [8]. An ACS can either be simulated or implemented in hardware. The idea of amorphous computing is to develop engineering techniques to control, organize, and exploit the behavior of a set of programmable computing particles [6].

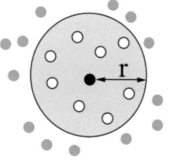

r = communication radius

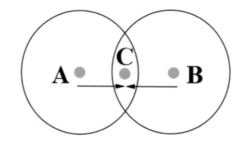

If A and B broadcast a message
at the same time, C will detect a collision

Figure 12.2 The communication model [6].

21.3 APPLICATIONS

The set of potential applications for amorphous computing is vast. Amorphous computing can deal with a variety of problems such as biology, sociology, computational geometry, self-reconfiguring computers or robot, cellular computing, logic system, sensor networks, MEMS, Internet nodes, programmable materials, smart paint, and smart materials. For example, smart materials involve mixing computational particles with bulk materials such as paint, gel, or concrete. The smart paint could be used to coat objects and then compute their shape, to sense the environment. Biological applications require nodes on sizes compatible with molecules or cells, which are complex and expensive to make using conventional top-down fabrication techniques.

21.4 BENEFITS AND CHALLENGES

A major motivation for studying amorphous computing is that the ability to program amorphous systems would greatly expand the set of physical substrates available to support in multicellular information processing [9]. Low design cost, board re-use, and flexibility were the initial attraction to amorphous computing systems. One of the interesting properties of amorphous computers is that they are robust with respect to the loss of individual processing units or elements. The ability to tailor a single board to diverse needs is advantageous where logistics and fault tolerance are concerned.

A completely functional amorphous computer has not yet been constructed. This is due to the fact silicon-based fabrication techniques (used for microelectronic processors) are not specifically built for use in an amorphous computer. To fabricate molecular-scale electronic structures may require cellular computing in conjunction with amorphous computing. Even if we can produce individual computing elements, the issue of how to program them still remains. Controlling an amorphous computer presents some serious challenges. Progress in amorphous computing may require new approaches to fault tolerance, which is achieved via redundancy rather than relying on hardware perfection.

21.5 CONCLUSION

Amorphous computing is a non-classical computing paradigm that relies on massively parallel computation by a large number of small elements weakly interacting together.

This is based on the existence of large numbers of inexpensive nodes with limited computational ability, limited memory capacity, and limited communication range. It is an emerging domain in computer science. It has attracted a great deal of interest among researchers both as an alternative computing model and as an inspiration to understand developmental biology. We are at early stage in the development of amorphous computing. More information about amorphous computing can be found in [10].

REFERENCES

[1] D. Chu, D. J. Barnes, and S. Perkins, "Amorphous computing in the presence of stochastic disturbances," *BioSystems*, vol. 25, 2014, pp. 32–42.

[2] "Amorphous computing," *Wikipedia*, the free encyclopedia, https://en.wikipedia.org/wiki/Amorphous_computing

[3] M. A. TerAvest, Z. Li and L. T. Angenent, "Bacteria-based biocomputing with cellular computing circuits to sense, decide, signal, and act," *Energy & Environmental Science*, vol. 12, 2011.

[4]   J. Wiedermann and L. Petru, "On the universal computing power of amorphous computing systems," *Theory of Computing System*, vol. 45, 2009, pp. 995–1010.

[5]   R. Nadpal and D. Coore, "An algorithm for group formation in an amorphous computer," *Proceedings of the 10ᵗʰ International Conference on Parallel and Distributed Systems,* 1998.

[6]   M. N. O. Sadiku, Y. Zhou, and S. M. Musa, "Amorphous Computing," *International Journal of Advances in Scientific Research and Engineering*, vol. 5, no. 4, April 2019, pp. 230-232.

[7]   J. Katzenelso, "Notes on amorphous computing," https://www.researchgate.net/publication/2242486_Notes_on_Amorphous_Computing

[8]   N. W. Anderson, "Amorphous computer system architecture: A preliminary look," *ACM SIGARCH Computer Architecture News*, vol. 18, no.1, March 1990.

[9]   H. Abelson et al., "Amorphous," *Communications of the ACM*, vol. 43, no. 5, May 2000, pp. 74-82.

[10] J. P. Banâtre et al.(eds.), *Unconventional Programming Paradigms*. Berlin, Germany: Springer-Verlag, 2005.

22
CHAPTER

SYMBOLIC COMPUTING

If you don't believe in the devil, it's because
you've never resisted him.
– Martin Luther

22.1 INTRODUCTION

Conducting scientific research via numerical computation is an established practice today. Computing is powerfully impacting the way that modern science and engineering are carried out. Symbolic computation refers to using machines or computers to manipulate mathematical equations and expressions in symbolic form, as opposed to numerical manipulation. Using symbolic computing to solve mathematical problems involves manipulations of symbolic objects, rules or programs, with the main goal of being exact. This is unlike most numeric calculations where computations use approximate floating point arithmetic.

Symbolic computing (or algebraic computing) is one of fastest growing areas of scientific computing. Since its earliest development in 1953, symbolic computing has increased in popularity and has been used in science, engineering, and other disciplines.

Symbolic computing is mainly concerned with the representation of information in symbolic form and how that information can be processed using computer systems. It allows solutions to be given exactly. Symbolic computing simplifies and streamlines calculation and reduces the potential for arithmetic error [1].

In contrast with numeric or conventional representation, symbolic computing deals with the representation and manipulation of information in symbolic form. Examples of numeric and symbolic computations are:

- Numeric multiplication: F = 6 * 5 = 30.
- Symbolic multiplication: $F = (2+j)*x_1*x_2*x_3 + x_1 + x_2 + 5*\sin(2*x_4)$

Symbolic computing can be used for symbolic integration or differentiation, substitution of one expression into another, simplification of an expression, etc. Symbolic computation requires large computational resources. It entails developing an infrastructure built upon massively distributed computational environments

This chapter provides a brief introduction to symbolic computing. It begins by explaining the concept of symbolic computing and showing how this style of computing differs from conventional computing. Then it discusses some examples, applications, benefits, and challenges of symbolic computing. The last section concludes with comments.

22.2 CONCEPT OF SYMBOLIC COMPUTING

In a nutshell, symbolic computing is a computer algorithm that requires input from the user in either numerical values or exact terms such as fractions, radicals, and symbols and then performs mathematical operations on the input. Both the input and output are symbolic. The tools for symbolic computations are standalone systems that require human interpretation and control. A symbolic computer has three major components: architectures, languages, and algorithms. Parallel computing requires co-ordinated evolution of these three components.

Since its earliest use in 1953, symbolic computing continues to gain popularity. Symbolic computing software has been used in advanced engineering applications. Today, users of symbolic computing systems include computer scientists, engineers, educators, and stock market analysts. Symbolic computers solve complex problems such as solving partial differential equations in science and engineering, probability functions for fractional ages, integrations for the Feymam diagrams in elementary particle physics, and problems in chemistry [2].

A key requirement in symbolic computation is to efficiently combine computer algebra systems (CASs) in order to be able to solve complex problems. Computer algebra overcomes the risk of obtaining incorrect results from algebraic manipulations. CAS has become the main tool for symbolic computations. Macsyma, developed at MIT, was one of the oldest CASs. Common examples of CAS are the Symbolic Computation Software Composability Protocol (SCSCP) and SymPy [3]. A computer algebra system stores mathematical expressions as data structures.

Languages commonly used for symbolic computing include FORTRAN, C, C++, Lisp, ML, Prolog, Python, and Java. Examples of symbolic algorithms include sorting, compiling, symbolic algebra, procedure calling, expert systems, and artificial intelligence systems.

22.3 EXAMPLES OF SYMBOLIC COMPUTING

One of the major successes in symbolic computation research has been the development of software systems. A representative example of software capable of performing symbolic computing is SymPy. SymPy is a computer algebra system (CAS) written in the Python, which is programming language that has a focus on ease of use and readability. It is a robust CAS which provides a wide spectrum of features in a wide range of scientific disciplines. Unlike several other CASs, SymPy does not attempt to develop and use its own programming language. Rather, it exclusively uses Python both as the internal language and the user language. This makes it easier for people already familiar with Python to use SymPy. All operations are performed symbolically. Symbolic variables or simply symbols, must be defined and assigned to Python variables. SymPy also supports matrices with symbolic dimension values. Computations on matrices with symbolic entries are necessary for many algorithms in SymPy. SymPy has equation solvers that can handle ordinary differential equations, recurrence relationships, and algebraic equations [4].

SymPy supports a wide range of mathematical facilities such as discrete math, concrete math, plotting, geometry, statistics, sets, series, vectors, combinatorics, group theory, code generation, tensors, simplifying expressions, performing common calculus operations, manipulating polynomials, pretty printing expressions, solving equations, precision numerics, and representing symbolic matrices. It also supports several higher mathematical functions such as gamma functions, Bessel functions, orthogonal polynomials, elliptic functions and integrals, zeta and polylogarithm functions, and generalized hypergeometric function [4]. The fact that SymPy is readable, free, and open source makes it attractive in spite of its limitations.

Another symbolic software is Maxima, which is a free and open-source CAS written in Lisp, and it can be downloaded from http://maxima.sourceforge.net [5]. It is a descendant of Macsyma, one of the oldest computer algebra systems developed at MIT in the 1960s.

22.4 APPLICATIONS

Symbolic computing is useful in different areas of mathematics such as computer algebra, linear algebra, computational logic, symbolic geometric methods, solution of algebraic equations, finite element simulations, equational theorem proving and rewriting, factorization of polynomials and operators, artificial intelligence, probabilistic and stochastic analysis, integration theory, chemical kinetic reaction, linguistic decision making, poor evolution pattern, and recurrence relation [6]. Some of these applications are explained in detailed below.

- *Mathematics:* Some of the most interesting applications of symbolic computing are in mathematics. Areas of both pure and applied mathematics, including coding theory, cryptography, probability theory, analysis, combinatorics, and number theory, have all benefited from the availability of the new symbolic computing tools. The main role of symbolic algebra systems is helping to formulate hypotheses and explore ramifications of mathematical models [7].
- *Finite Element Simulations:* Several problems in science and engineering are formulated as systems of partial differential equations, which can be solved using a numerical technique such as finite element method. Finite element codes can be generated from a symbolic specification of the mathematical problem. The specifications of the model, i.e. PDEs, boundary and initial conditions, are entered into Maple, since Maple worksheet automatically provides a readable and complete documentation [8].
- *Linguistic Decision Making:* Decision problems usually require that human beings provide their knowledge or preferences about a set of different alternatives to make a decision by means of reasoning processes. The use of linguistic information dictates the need to operate with linguistic variables. Its computational model provides accurate results because they are represented by means of a linguistic term and a numerical value [9].
- *The Efficient Score:* The efficient score test is applicable to a wide variety of data types and models. Symbolic computing offers a convenient means of addressing the major drawback of using the efficient score, i.e., the sometimes arduous derivation of the score function. It simplifies the derivation of the efficient score and eliminates error due to manual derivations [10].

Whatever the application, users have a variety of symbolic processors to choose from. These include MAPLE, MATHEMATICA, MATHCAD, and MAXIMA., Functional programming and logic programming are two common applications of symbolic computing. To functional programming, *pure* functions are the basic unit of computation and they are entirely characterized by the results they return for a given set of arguments. To logic programming, logical predicates are the basic unit of computation and a predicate is defined as a true relationship [11].

Symbolic computing applications may run in isolation or as components of larger systems. They may be integrated to perform a broader function.

22.5 BENEFITS AND CHALLENGES

The main benefit of using symbolic computing is producing an exact result. Symbolic computation has been used extensively in developing closed form solutions to engineering problems. It provides the opportunity to handle algebraic expressions that previously may have reached "unmanageable proportions." The use of symbolic computational software improves the reliability of calculations as well as provides a means of shortening the time required to perform extensive and repetitive calculations. It has been observed that the use of symbolic computational improves the reliability of calculations as well as provides a method to shorten the time required for performing extensive and repetitive calculations [12].

Development of symbolic computing has been slow until recently due to the inadequacy of available computational resources such computer memory and processor power. Now a variety of symbolic computing software packages are available for engineering use. Also, computer algebra systems (CASs) are now capable of solving large problems such as the Grid [13]. Symbolic computations are hard to parallelize due to their complex data and control structures. They requires large computational resources.

22.6 CONCLUSION

Symbolic computing emphasizes *exact* computation with exactly represented data and with expressions containing variables that are manipulated as symbols. Scientific research via symbolic computation is less widespread than other techniques. However, with the advent of time-sharing and virtual memory operating systems, research on symbolic computation have flourished. Notable, impressive results have been achieved in symbolic computation over the last two decades [14]. Symbolic computation has made mathematics more useful to other scientific fields. It is now routinely used in a number of diverse disciplines such as mathematical research, physics, engineering, education, and economic. The needs for symbolic computation have grown.

Universities should introduce symbolic computation as a tool into thier existing courses. An attempt to teach undergraduate courses in computer graphics and robotics using symbolic computing systems has been made [15]. For additional information on symbolic computing, one should consult books in [16-23] and the journal exclusively devoted to it: *Journal of Symbolic Computation*.

REFERENCES

[1] A. B. Sibley et al., "Facilitating the calculation of the efficient score using symbolic computing," *The American Statistician*, vol. 72, no. 2, 2018, pp. 199-205.

[2] F. Y. Chan, "Symbolic computing," *Insurance: Mathematics and Economics*, vol. 6, 1987, pp. 203-212.

[3]   S. Lintona et al., "Easy composition of symbolic computation software using SCSCP: A new lingua franca for symbolic computation," *Journal of Symbolic Computation*, vol. 49, 2013, pp. 95-122.

[4]   A. Meurer et al.,"SymPy: symbolic computing in Python," *PeerJ Preprints,* June 2016. https://github.com/sympy/sympy-paper.

[5]   G. L. Lo Magno, "More power through symbolic computation: Extending stata by using the Maxima computer algebra system," *The Stata Journal*, vol.15, no. 1, 2015, pp. 45–76.

[6]   F. Winkler, "What can symbolic computation contribute to mathematics?" *Proceedings of the 13th International Symposium on Symbolic and Numeric Algorithms for Scientific Computing*, 2011, pp. 19-20.

[7]   A. Boyle and B. F. Caviness (eds.), *Future Directions for Research in Symbolic Computation.* Philadelphia, PA: Society for Industrial and Applied Mathematics, 1990, p.40.

[8]   G. Amberg, R. Tonhardt, and C. Winkler, "Finite element simulations using symbolic computing," *Mathematics and Computers in Simulation,* vol. 49, 1999, pp. 257-274.

[9]   R. M. Rodrıguez and L. Martınez, "An analysis of symbolic linguistic computing models in decision making," *International Journal of General Systems*, vol. 42, no. 1, January 2013, pp. 121–136.

[10]   A. B. Sibley et al., "Facilitating the calculation of the efficient score using symbolic computing," *The American Statistician*, vol. 72, no. 2, 2018, pp. 199-205.

[11]   A. M. Oteniya, M. N. O. Sadiku, and S. M. Musa, "Symbolic Computing," *International Journal of Scientific and Research Publications*, vol. 10, no. 3, March 2020, pp. 158-162.

[12]   E. L. Richards, "Application of symbolic computing in analysis of modal properties of structurally coupled twin tall buildings," *M. Sc. Thesis,* Colorado State University Fort Collins, Colorado, Spring 2011.

[13]   D. Petcu, "Distributed symbolic computations," *Proceedings of the Sixth International Symposium on Parallel and Distributed Computing,* July 2007

[14]   A. Boyle and B. F. Caviness, "Future directions for research in symbolic computation," April, 1988 https://www.eecis.udel.edu/~caviness/wsreport.pdf

[15]   K. Sridharan, "Teaching computer graphics and robotics using symbolic computation software," *Symbolic Computation Software,* 2000, pp. 18-30.

[16]   Frank E. Harris, *Mathematics for Physical Science and Engineering: Symbolic Computing, Applications in Maple and Mathematica.* Academic Press, 2014.

[17]   B. Harvey, *Computer Science Logo Style. Volume 1 Symbolic Computing.* Cambridge, MA: The MIT Press, 2nd ed., 1997.

[18]   D. S. Touretzky, *COMMON LISP: A Gentle Introduction to Symbolic Computation.* Redwood City, CA: The Benjamin/Cummings Publishing Company, 1990.

[19]   U. Langer and P. Paule (eds.), *Numerical and Symbolic Scientific Computing: Progress and Prospects.* Springer, 2012.

[20]   E.G. Rajan, *Symbolic Computing : Signal and Image Processing.* Anshan, 2005.

[21]   R. A. Mueller and R. L. Page, *Symbolic Computing With Lisp And Prolog.* Wiley, 1988.

[22]   J. S. Cohen, *Computer Algebra and Symbolic Computation: Mathematical Methods.* Natick, MA: A. K. Peters, 2003.

[23]   Z. A. Karian, *Symbolic Computation in Undergraduate Mathematics Education.* Mathematical Association of America, 1992.

23

INTERNET COMPUTING

It is a profound error to presume that everything has been discovered; it is to
take the horizon which bounds the eye for the limit of the world.
- A. M. Lemirre

23.1 INTRODUCTION

Computing is any activity that involves using computers. It is any goal-oriented activity requiring the use of computers. It includes designing and building hardware and software systems for a wide range of purposes [1]. The Internet is the largest network which connects a large number of smaller computer networks such as those owned by universities, industries, nonprofit organizations, and governments. The phenomenal growth of the Internet has connected us to a vast amount of computation resources around the globe.

The Internet is a global computer network that uses the standard Internet protocol suite (TCP/IP) to serve billions of users. It is a gigantic sized network of networks, which provides software/hardware infrastructure to establish and maintain connectivity of the computers around the world. The internet is a central feature of society which permeates nearly all economic and social activities. The ever-growing popularity of the Internet and the wide-acceptance of the World Wide Web have motivated numerous research works leading to various computing schemes such as cloud computing and Internet computing [2].

Internet computing represents a new way of designing and developing information systems. It is essentially a large scale distributed computing which involves workstations from different management domains on the Internet. It is a new type of distributed computing which involves heterogeneous workstations from different organizations on the Internet. It has resulted in deep changes in infrastructures and development practices of computing. It is a critically important, integral component of modern life.

With Internet computing, all a user needs is a standard web browser. The proliferation of the devices connected to the Internet brings the distributed computation resources and information resources all together into a huge network. In order to effectively use this huge network, many research issues have been studied.

This chapter provides a brief introduction to Internet computing. It begins by discussing the basic features of Internet computing. Then it discusses the applications, benefits, and challenges of Internet computer. The last section concludes with some comments.

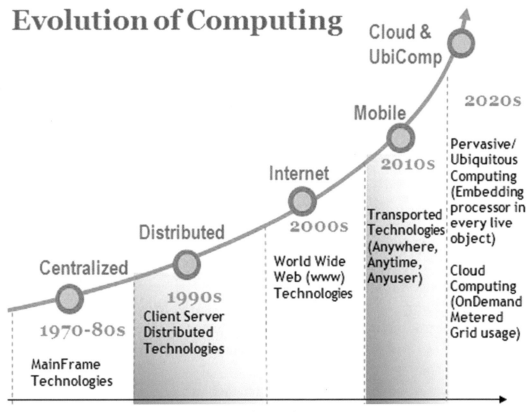

Figure 23.1 Evolution of computing [4].

23.2 CONCEPT OF INTERNET COMPUTING

In the late 1960s, two computers could communicate with each other through a computer network. In the early 1980s the TCP/IP suite was introduced. Commercial use of the Internet began in the late 1980s. The World Wide Web (WWW) became available in 1991 which made the Internet more popular [3]. Over the Internet, different users share their computing resources, and computations take place in a distributed manner. Internet computing shares the goal of better utilizing existing computing resources. It promises to fulfill the vision of "anytime" "anywhere" computing. Figure 23.1 shows the evolution of computing [4].

There are five underlying principles we can use to define Internet computing [5]:

- Computation (algorithms, complexity, and the like)
- Communication (such as Shannon entropy and data transmission)
- Coordination (human computer and computer-computer interfaces)
- Automation (artificial intelligence and machine learning)
- Recollection (storage hierarchies and search)

The most basic Internet computing principle is about communication — the transfer of information over a distance. The communication may be about people and protocols.

Application software, popular known as an an "app," is a computer software designed to help the user to perform specific tasks. Java is becoming the language of choice for Internet computing for two simple reasons: security and platform independence [6].

23.3 APPLICATIONS

The Internet is a global network which permeates nearly all economic and social activities. Internet computing is applied is various areas such Internet-based computing, e-business, information system, smart cards, and optimization

- *Internet-based Technologies:* Commonly known applications of Internet computing are Internet of things (IoT), cloud computing, cloud of things (CoT), and cooperative computing. The Internet of things (IoT), which is a worldwide network of physical objects using the Internet as a communication network. The Internet has changed everything and provided "smartness" to these connected things. IoT is the Internet of the future and it will seriously impact our life [7]. Cloud computing is a new field in Internet computing. Cloud computing is internet computing whereby shared resources, software, and information are provided to computers and other devices on demand similar to an electric power grid. The key driving forces behind cloud computing are the promise of wireless networking ubiquity, lower storage, and progressive improvements in Internet computing software, and mobile computing [8]. IoT and cloud computing working together in integration makes a new paradigm, known as Cloud of Things (CoT) or Cloud of Everything [9]. The cloud of things allows you to automate your operations easily and effectively. Cooperative computing represents the convergence of two important inter-related technologies, namely, the Internet and the support of co-operation among a number of users in a concurrent manner.
- *E-business:* Internet computing provides the foundation on which e-business runs. It deploys all business applications across the Internet. It is the only architecture that can run all facets of business and support all information flows over the Internet. With Internet computing, all a user needs is a standard Web browser. An Internet computing architecture provides universal access to every person, scalability to support retailers of any size, and simplified distribution of critical business information across the enterprise [10].
- *Information System* (IS): This is a novel organizational application of digital computer and information communication technologies (ICT). Organizational computing has entered an era of Internet computing, which has led to new techniques and practices that collectively represent a distinct way of conceiving and developing IS. For an IS innovation enabled by an architectural shift to be disruptive, it must be both radical and pervasive [11]

23.4 BENEFITS AND CHALLENGES

Internet computing provides the opportunity to form virtual computers with gigantic processing power. It also offers the potential of selling and buying surplus computing power over the Internet [12]. It supports scalability at a much lower cost. Today people should embrace Internet computing because it is the way to compete in the Internet era.

Internet computing is always considered to be complex due to its nature of distributed, largescale, and high communication latency. The Internet is loosely coupled and has no global administration. Fault tolerance measures are always required for building Internet computing system. The collaboration among Internet users is difficult due to the inherent heterogeneous nature of the computation resources [13]. The challenge of designing distributed programs that run across the Internet is always modularization—figuring out where to do what. Since millions of Internet users communicate with each other, share resources, and exchange sensitive data, security is greatly needed to guarantee confidence in service providers.

23.5 CONCLUSION

The Internet has been growing exponentially for the past few years and this phenomenal growth will continue. As Internet technologies become mature, more and more enterprises will be attracted to the cost-effectiveness of Internet-based applications.

Internet computing is all about a huge network computing system based on the information resources available world-wide across the Internet. It has been regarded as a major revolutionary change in computing. Embracing Internet computing is the right way to compete in the new millennium. More information on Internet computing can be found in books in [14-17] and the journal exclusively devoted to it: *IEEE Internet Computing*.

REFERENCES

[1] "Computing," *Wikipedia*, the free encyclopedia https://en.wikipedia.org/wiki/Computing

[2] M. N. O. Sadiku, P. O. Adebo, S. M. Musa, "Internet Computing," *International Journal of Advanced Research in Computer Science and Software Engineering*, vol. 9, no. 3, March 2019, pp. 53-55.

[3] C. Perera et al., "Context aware computing for the Internet of things: A survey," *IEEE Communications Surveys & Tutorials*, vol. 16, no. 1, First Quarter 2014, pp. 414-454.

[4] V. Madurai, "Ubiquitous computing," https://medium.com/@vivekmadurai/ubiquitous-computing-6dd3685f18e7

[5] R. E. Filman, "Internet computing," *IEEE Internet Computing,* Nov. – Dec. 2005, pp. 4-6.

[6] S. B. Guthery, "Java card: Internet computing on a smart card," *IEEE Internet Computing*, Jan.-Feb. 1997, pp. 57-59.

[7] M. N. O. Sadiku, *Emerging Internet-based Technologies*. Boca Raton, FL: CRC Press, 2019.

[8] G. Pallis, "Cloud computing: The new frontier of Internet computing," *IEEE Internet Computing,* Sept.-Oct. 2010, pp. 70-73.

[9] A. M. Oteniya, M. N. O. Sadiku, and S. M. Musa, "Cloud of things: A primer," *International Journal of Trend in Research and Development*, vol. 5, no. 6, Nov.-Dec. 2018, pp. 284-286.

[10] "How to define Internet computing," https://www.supplychainmarket.com/doc/how-to-define-internet-computing-0001

[11] K. Lyytinen and G. M. Rose, "Disruptive information system innovation: The case of Internet computing," *Info Systems Journal,* vol. 13, 2003, pp. 301–330.

[12] Y. Y. Wong, K. S. Leung, and K. H. Le, "A stochastic load balancing algorithm for i-computing," *Concurrency snd Computation: Practice and Experience Concurrency*, vol. 15, 2003, pp. 55–57.

[13] L. Yan, "Internet computing with distributed software agent," *Doctoral Dissertation,* Florida International University, 2000.

[14] M. P. Singh (ed.), *The Practical Handbook of Internet Computing*. Boca Raton, FL: Chapman & Hall/CRC Press, 2005.

[15] F. Xhafa, L. Barolli, and F. Amato (eds.), *Advances on P2P, Parallel, Grid, Cloud and Internet Computing.* Springer, 2017.

[16] D. Zhang, X. Li, and Z. Liu, *Parallel Processing for Image Restoration. In: Data Management and Internet Computing for Image/Pattern Analysis.* Boston, MA: Springer, 2001.

[17] A. Rocus (ed.), *Internet Computing: Technologies, Frameworks and Applications.* ML Books International, 2016.

24

CHAOS COMPUTING

Discovery consists of looking at the same thing as everyone else does and thinking something different.
- Albert Szent-Gyorgyi

24.1 INTRODUCTION

Computing for the last fifty years is based on Moore's law, which is now delivering diminishing returns. Modern digital computers perform computations based upon digital logic gates, which are essentially seven: AND, OR, NOT, NAND, NOR, XOR and XNOR. There has been interest in so called alternative or unconventional computing paradigms that differ from traditional silicon-based computing architectures. One such paradigms is chaos computing [1].

Chaos computing is a new unconventional paradigm for computing, where chaotic oscillators are used for computation. The word "chaos" commonly means a state of disorder, the existence of random behavior, utter confusion or disorganization. In mathematics, chaos signifies that the equations expressing nonlinear systems are extremely sensitive to initial inputs or conditions and it is hardly possible to predict their future behavior with a high degree of certainty [2]. Chaos computing is based on the nonlinear dynamical principles and can perform all logical operations. It aims at implementing computing functions through construction of logical gates by employing chaotic elements.

This chapter provides an introduction to chaos computing. It begins with understanding of the concept of chaos. It then covers the unique fundamental features of chaos computing. It addresses some benefits and challenges of chaos computing. The last section concludes with some comments.

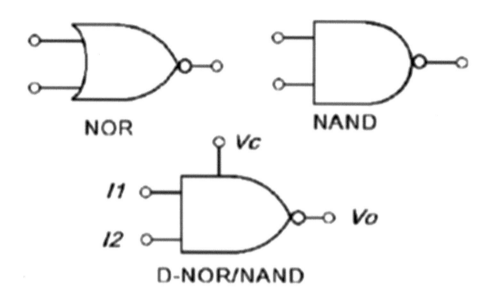

Figure 24.1 Symbols for NOR, NAND and dynamic-NOR/NAND logic gates [7].

24.2 CONCEPT OF CHAOS

Chaos theory is an integral component of science, mathematics, art, and computing. The study of chaotic systems (or chaos in short) has attracted much attention in recent years. Chaos is defined mathematically as any irregular behavior which results from the application of a fixed set of rules. It is a random-seeming behavior generated by deterministic systems. Chaos is all around us. It is found in many disciplines, such as physics, chemistry, biology, medicine, and engineering. For example, chaotic phenomena are found in lasers, electronic circuits, chemical systems, weather forecasting, and biomedical problems such as the analysis of the brains and hearts.

Chaos is not really unpredictabe. Chaotic systems can behave in a predictable and reproducible way (given the same initial conditions). However, the evolution of a chaotic system depends largely on its starting conditions, which leads to a behavior that is ultimately unpredictable [3]. In real life, we cannot know the exact value of the initial conditions of a system.

Edward Lorenz from MIT is famously regarded as a "founding father" of chaos. Chaos has three defining characteristics [4]: (1) sensitivity to initial conditions, (2) aperiodic long-term behavior, and (3) it is wholly deterministic. Chaotic behavior is manifested in many natural systems, such as lasers, neurons in the brain, electronic circuits, chemical systems, weather, and road traffic.

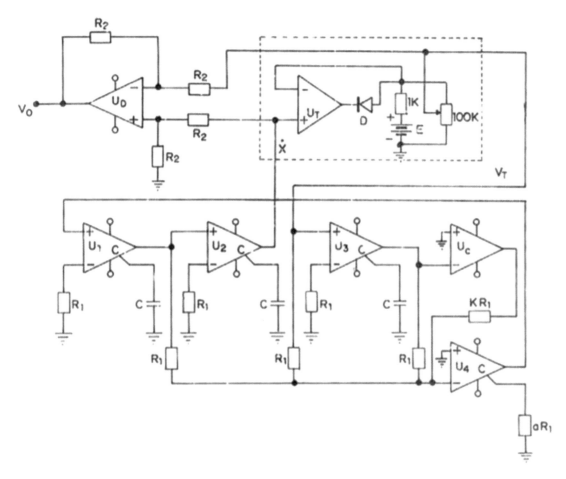

Figure 24.2 A typical circuit model for implementing NOR gate [8].

24.3 BASICS OF CHAOS COMPUTING

Chaos computing uses chaotic systems for computation. Chaotic systems can be made to produce all types of logic gates. By controlling how inputs are mapped to outputs, a specific task can be performed. Chaotic computer can directly perform basic numerical operations like addition and multiplication. Research has shown how chaotic computers can be recruited in fault tolerant applications by introducing dynamic based fault detection methods [5]. A chaotic system enables us to build better computers that have a flexible instruction set and carry out computation that conventional computers are not good at.

The term "chaos computing" was introduced in 1975 by the US mathematicians Tien lien Li and James A. Yorke in their ground breaking paper, "Period Three Implies Chaos." They introduced a new direction to computing using nonlinear chaotic dynamics. The term "chaos computing" was popularized by William Ditto of the Georgia Institute of Technology, who believes that the unpredictabilty of chaotic processes may power a new breed of computer. Ditto's chip is like the microelectronic version of a stem cell that can assume all sorts of different functions.

Chaos computing provides a new approach to implementing a logic circuit. It takes advantage of the richness of nonlinear dynamical systems and insights from neural systems to devise new approaches to create a chaos-based computer. Nonlinear dynamics has revealed a rich array of behaviors, especially those related to chaos including routes to chaos, high and low dimensional chaotic attractors, and transient chaos. In neural systems, measured phenomena include chaos, synchrony, and cascading avalanches demonstrating that information processing in the brain is not just anatomical, but also dynamical

A system is capable of serving as a universal general purpose computing provided it can emulate all logic gates. Using single chaotic element, each logical operation (AND, OR, NOT, NAND, NOR, XOR) can be realized [6]. Figure 24.1 shows the symbols for NOR, NAND and Dynamic-NOR/NAND logic gates [7]. A typical circuit for realizing NOR gate is shown in Figure 24.2 [8]. Computer memory can be constructed by combining logical gates. Chaotic computer can not only implement logic functions, they can perform basic numerical operations like addition and multiplication. Although chaotic computers are irregular, they very organized.

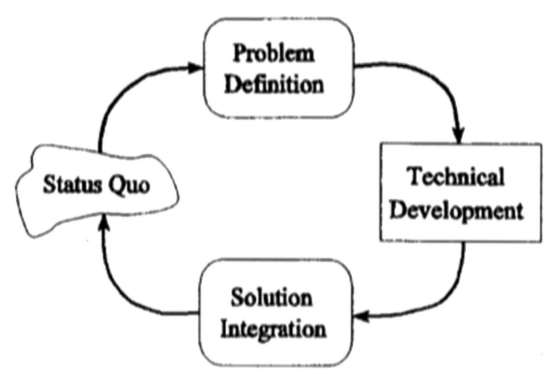

Figure 24.3 The phases of the linear problem-solving loop [9].

24.4 APPLICATIONS

The chaos-based computer can be applied to problems in generic computation, DNA computing, modeling speech, speech processing, pattern recognition, voice recognition, controller for autonomous vehicles, quantum computing, and robotic platforms. Chao computing can also be implemented in specialized domains such as a biological environment and nano fluidics. The following represent just a few applications of chao computing.

- *Software Development*: This is a human activity since people write and use software. Creating software is very complex. The chaos model combines a linear problem-solving loop with fractals to describe the complexity of software development. As shown in Figure 24.3, the linear problem-solving loop involves four different stages: problem definition, technical development, solution integration, and status quo. Software development is the flow from one project state to the next [9].

- *Encrypted Computation*: Current schemes for encrypted computation all use essentially the same "noisy" approach: they encrypt via a noisy encoding of the message. Although the noisy approach "works," using chaotic system can improve its efficiency [10].

24.5 BENEFITS AND CHALLENGES

A reconfigurable chaos-based computer will be of great benefit to military and civilian customers because reuse of logic morphable gates can led to fewer logic gates and lower cooling requirements. The major benefit of a chaotic system is that it enables us to: (1) build better computers that have a flexible instruction set, and (2) carry out computation that conventional computers are not good at [11]. In other words, chaos computing allows the same circuit to be programmed to implement different types of computation. Other major potential advantages of chaos computing include high speed, low power, low cost, a general-purpose form of computing, dynamic logical architecture, implementation of continuous logic, robustness against noise, and parallel and distributed computing [12].

Using chaos based logic provides opportunities for building computing systems with similar hardware but different configurations of operation. A completely different circuit could be implemented on the same hardware. Chaos based architectures can help us avoid trillion dollar research and development that has only marginal gains. Novel chaos computing can lead to new paradigms for the optimization of solving complex problems, such as controllers for autonomous systems, including robots and vehicles. The chaos computing chip can be fabricated using conventional technology.

A number of challenges may hinder the development of practical chaos-based computers. One major challenge for developing chaos-based computers is that the overhead associated with the physical implementation of a chaotic gate is quite higher than an equivalent digital gate [13].

24.6 CONCLUSION

Chaos computing is an unconventional computing paradigm that exploits the non-linearity of chaotic systems. The dynamic chaotic computer can perform computations and is promising because of its flexibility for changing logic gates by slightly modifying its parameter values. Chaos computing is still in its infancy. Chaos computing/theory remains an active area of research that involves several disciplines including mathematics, natural sciences (physics, biology, and chemistry), psychology, meteorology, and robotics.

More information on chaos computing can be found in the books in [14-16] and the journal that is exclusively devoted to it: *International Journal of Chaotic Computing.*

REFERENCES

[1]   M. N. O. Sadiku, A. E. Shadare, and S. M. Musa, "Chaos computing: An introduction," *International Journal of Engineering Research and Advanced Technology,* vol. 5, no. 4, April 2019, pp. 16-18.

[2]   "Chaos theory," *Wikipedia,* the free encyclopedia
https://en.wikipedia.org/wiki/Chaos_theory

[3]   "Logic from chaos?"

https://www.economist.com/science-and-technology/2004/04/01/logic-from-chaos

[4]   D. Kuo, "Chaos and its computing paradigm," *IEEE Potentials*, April/May 2006, pp. 13-15.

[5]   "Chaos computing," *Wikipedia*, the free encyclopedia
      https://en.wikipedia.org/wiki/Chaos_computing

[6]   T. Munakata, S. Sinha, and W. L. Ditto, "Chaos computing: Implementation of fundamental logical
      gates by chaotic elements," *IEEE Transactions on Circuits and Systems—I: Fundamental Theory and
      Applications,* vol. 49, no. 11, November 2002, pp. 1629-1633.

[7]   W. L. Ditto, K. Murali, and S. Sinha, "Chaos computing: Ideas and implementations," The 9th
      Experimental Chaos Conference, Sao Paulo, Brazil, May - June, 2006.

[8]   K. Murali, S. Sinha, and I. R. Mohamed, "Chaos computing: Experimental realization of NOR
      gate using a simple chaotic circuit." *Physics Letters A*, vol. 339, 2005, pp. 39-44.

[9]   L B. S. Raccoon. "The chaos model and the chaos life cycle," *ACM SIGSOFT Software Engineering
      Notes,* vol. 20, no. 1, January 1995, pp. 55-66.

[10] C. Gentry, "Computing on the edge of chaos: Structure and randomness in encrypted computation,"
      Proceedings of the International Congress of Mathematicians, Seoul, 2014, pp. 609-632.

[11] B. Kia, "Chaos computing: From theory to application," *Doctoral Dissertation*, Arizona State
      University, December 2011.

[12] T. Munakata et al., "Chaos computing: A unified view," *International Journal of Parallel, Emergent
      and Distributed Systems*, vol. 25, no. 1, February 2010, pp. 3-16.

[13] B. Majumder et al., "Chaos computing for mitigating side channel attack," *Proceedings on IEEE
      International Symposium on Hardware Oriented Security and Trust,* April-May 2018, pp. 143-146.

[14] L. Kocarev, Z. Galias, and S. Lian (eds.), *Intelligent Computing Based on Chaos*. Berlin: Springer, 2009.

[15] E. Schöll and H.G. Schuster (eds.), *Handbook of Chaos Control*. John Wiley & Sons, 2008.

[16] A. T. Azar and S. Vaidyanathan (eds.), *Advances in Chaos Theory and Intelligent Control*. Springer, 2016.

INDEX

V

Virtual reality, 11

W

Watson, 93,94
Wearable computers, 102

Wetware computer, 82
Wi-Fi, 107,109
Wireless, 122
Wireless communication, 108

Z

Zadeh, Lofti A., 61